# THE MODERN BOOK OF FENG SHUI

## VITALITY AND HARMONY FOR THE HOME AND OFFICE

# THE MODERN BOOK OF FENG SHUI
## VITALITY AND HARMONY FOR THE HOME AND OFFICE

BY STEVEN POST • PHOTOGRAPHS BY MERT CARPENTER

A BYRON PREISS BOOK

A DELL TRADE PAPERBACK

A BYRON PREISS BOOK

Published by Dell Publishing
a division of Bantam Doubleday Dell
Publishing Group, Inc.
1540 Broadway
New York, NY 10036

The Modern Book of Feng Shui: Vitality and Harmony for the Home and Office
by Steven Post; Photographs by Mert Carpenter

A Byron Preiss Book
Library of Congress Cataloging in Publication Data

Post, Steven.
The modern book of feng shui: vitality and harmony for the home
and office / by Steven Post.
p.   cm.
ISBN 0-440-50768-5
1. Feng shui.   I. Title.
SF1779.F4P67   1998
133.3'336—dc21                          97-44961
                                          CIP

Printed in the United States of America
Published simultaneously in Canada
April 1998
10 9 8 7 6 5 4 3
FFG

# THIS BOOK IS DEDICATED TO PROFESSOR THOMAS LIN YUN A LIVING BUDDHA

Professor Thomas Lin Yun was the first Chinese master willing to openly disclose the secrets of the art of Feng Shui and to train students in the West. Through his indefatigable teaching and worldwide travels, Professor Lin has popularized Feng Shui internationally. I met him in his first public class in the late Seventies in the United States and have been his student ever since.

Regarded as a "living Buddha," Professor Lin has great knowledge, insight into life, and personal power. His understanding of the *chi* he encounters makes him among the most impressive human beings I have met. People travel from around the world to ask his help. The confidant of heads of state, leaders in business, education, and the arts, he is called *Erge,* or Second Brother, by his disciples, symbolizing his availability, kindness, and profound skillfulness.

Of the Five Constant Virtues of traditional Chinese culture, the virtue associated with the element Wood is *jen,* often translated as kindness, humanity, goodness, or human heartedness. *Jen* is a compound of "two" and "man." Like the English words "kind" (which derives from "kin," or family) and "gentle" (from the Latin *gens,* or clan), *jen* emphasizes the relationship among people. *Jen* has been called the virtue of the soul, which helps establish union and harmony among people. It makes the Tao present in human society. *Jen,* also, can literally mean seeds—the seeds in the stones of peaches and apricots, which, after being sown in the soil, will sprout and grow, showing how all things spring into life. Of Professor Lin, whose name (Lin) means a grove of trees, we may say: The seed of kindness has become a forest.

## AUTHOR'S SPECIAL THANKS:

I give my deepest thanks to Professor Lin Yun, Sifu Kuo Lien Ying, and my other masters and teachers. My wife Brenda Schuman-Post, my children Molly Rose and Elijah, and my beloved parents Birdie and Louis Post have given me precious inspiration and support. My GEO partners Edgar Sung and Barry Gordon have provided invaluable advice. Special thanks, as well to Cindy Chan and Manuela Jemma, to Julie Han of GEO, to Mert Carpenter and Margaret at Carpenter Photography, to my clients, students, friends, and to those who made their homes, workplaces, or persons available for photographs, and to my editor, Dinah Dunn, for her encouragement, clarity, and publishing brilliance.

The author wishes to especially thank Mrs. Jean Hanavan for permission to photograph her remarkable home, which was designed by GEO co-founder Edgar Sung, who used his expertise in Feng Shui to fashion a beautiful dwelling that combines ancient and modern elements to create balance, harmony, comfort, and delight.

# CONTENTS

# FOREWORD
## BY PROFESSOR THOMAS LIN YUN
### TRANSLATED BY JULIA HSU AND MARY HSU

Some twenty-five years ago, not only did Westerners find the topics of Feng Shui and geomancy very unfamiliar; even Easterners who had been living overseas might have been unfamiliar with the art. Today in Europe and the United States, the study of Feng Shui is no longer a novelty. In many magazines and even small local newspapers, one frequently finds articles or advertisements related to Feng Shui. Of these, the majority are written by Westerners who research Eastern subjects or are connected with research centers that study Eastern Feng Shui. Now there are even Western Feng Shui and Geomancy experts who offer consultation and suggestions to those in need and teach them how to apply Feng Shui to increase happiness in their lives.

Among the Feng Shui experts who have assisted in the development of a peaceful society is Steven Post, whom I have known for over twenty years, and who my disciples and I respect very much. Steven sent me his original manuscript as a gift and asked me to write a foreword for *The Modern Book of Feng Shui*. He also requested that I write some Chinese calligraphies to help illustrate key concepts and to bless his readers, which you find in this book.

I did not need to read Steven's manuscript to know that the content of the book must be very educational, substantial, and accurate. His scholastic attitude was evident early in our relationship by his listening skills and study habits throughout my workshops and lectures.

I have attended Steven's lectures, and I have been pleased to note that he is able to use everyday language in explaining his profound knowledge. He is an esteemed scholar who is familiar with both ancient and modern studies. When he presents his scholastic views, he quotes from classic writings and the most reliable sources, thus making his analysis honest, dependable, and accurate. His Feng Shui studies are not limited to the Eastern or the Chinese. His scholastic attainment in the geomancy of the ancient world and the world's religions is also impressively remarkable. His knowledge of Chinese Feng Shui is deep and very profound, including the traditional, the non-traditional, Black Sect Tantric Buddhist School, non-Black Sect Tantric Buddhist schools, Taoist School, exoteric Buddhist School, Yin-Yang School, and Eclectic School. Of the many educational institutions now established, Steven Post, Edgar Sung, and Barry Gordon of GEO are the foremost promoters. GEO (Geomancy/Feng Shui Education Organization), of which Steven is the CEO, has educated numerous Feng Shui experts who have made a tremendous contribution to society.

Steven has also traveled to China many times with me and Professor Leo Chen, the supreme supervisor of the Fourth Stage of Black Sect Tantric Buddhism, noted scholar, and superintendent of the Lin Yun Temple. During our visits, Steven gave expert Feng Shui analyses and transcendental adjustment methods for China's major cities, townships, streets, residences, ancient temples, airports, seaports, and boundaries.

Steven's vast knowledge, abundance of experiences, and spiritual cultivation all indicate to me that, had I not read his manuscript, I could assume that any book he has written must be of excellent standards and would be extremely influential. I was not disappointed. The content of *The Modern Book of Feng Shui* is indeed rich, the analysis very detailed, and the transcendental solutions are truly accurate. His careful presentation begins with the philosophy of Feng Shui, including tai chi, yin-yang, Eight Trigrams, and Five Elements. More importantly, he has revealed the unshared secrets exclusive to Black Sect Tantric, including the Three Secret Reinforcements and the Method of Minor Additions, a process that allows for Feng Shui adjustments without changing residence or renovating your house. In addition he uses many reports and analyses based on actual case studies.

In Part I, Steven clarifies the differences and similarities between ancient Feng Shui and its modern counterpart; introduces the practical side of Feng Shui from the perspective of Black Sect Tantric Buddhism, especially the applications of transcendental solutions, the Eight Trigrams, the mouth of *chi*, the three door *ba kua* method, and the representation and meaning of each trigram; and conveys how to adjust for missing or enhanced trigrams. He also explains the theory of the Five Elements and its practical application for exteriors, interiors, and choice of clothing color. In his description of the Method of Minor Additions, Steven focuses on how to adjust Feng Shui by using light, sound, life, dynamic processes, weight, representations of power, color, and so forth.

Part II of this book is even more exciting. All the concepts of Black Sect Tantric Buddhist Feng Shui are introduced clearly, including the objective, tangible versus the intangible dimension; how to adjust *chi*; interior decoration; and how Feng Shui influences one's working environment.

Steven familiarizes reader with personal *chi* enhancing adjustments in Part III. He imparts the special method of how to create the precious treasure box in order to increase one's wealth, longevity, luck, and safety. In addition, he has described secret methods that I have handed down to obtain a successful and happy marriage, and how to travel safely.

For those new to Feng Shui, as well as Feng Shui experts, a careful reading of Steven's book will provide unimaginable benefits. If you bought this book but were unable to find the time to read it, the good-hearted author's hard work, time, and spirit would be wasted. If you saw this book but did not purchase it, then you would lose the good karma of your life, for this book has been specially blessed and contains various mantra. According to folk beliefs, any object blessed with mantra should be treated as if gods and Buddhas are with it and that object can be used to guard residence and ward off evil. An old Chinese proverb states: Open the book and you benefit! If you open this book, you will be greatly benefited. I give *The Modern Book of Feng Shui* my strongest commendation.

In 1970 I moved from New York City to the San Francisco Bay area specifically to visit Mount Tamalpais in Marin County. I was drawn to this sacred mountain, which in traditional Feng Shui terms is the Root Support, the Support of Heaven, or Back Rest for much of the bay area. I became a Fire Lookout on Mount Tamalpais in 1972 and, at that time, made a formal commitment to learn everything I could about Feng Shui, geomancy, earth mysteries, and related subjects. In those days, if I said, "Feng Shui," to a non-Chinese speaker, the response might have been, "God bless you!"

Twenty-five years later, due primarily to its popularization in the United States by Professor Thomas Lin Yun, Feng Shui (pronounced FUNG SHWAY) is gaining widespread acceptance and moving into the mainstream. Feng Shui, the ancient Chinese art of placement, has become an influence to reckon with in contemporary culture. In the construction and interior design of skyscrapers and the homes of the rich and famous, savvy investors, builders, and corporate planners increasingly take advantage of Feng Shui in deciding where to build, what to build or buy, and how to arrange the details. Many Americans are interested in how they can use this art in their own lives, homes, and workplaces.

Feng Shui can unite our compassion, skillful action, and wisdom with the Path of Life, the Tao. Feng Shui harmonizes us with *chi*, the vital energy of all creation, to help us live better. This book will enable you to develop an understanding of Feng Shui and how to create a foundation of knowledge upon which to apply the techniques of this art. As you move through this book, from principles to techniques which you can practice, I hope that the blessings of good Feng Shui will fill your life.

# INTRODUCTION TO FENG SHUI

THE ROOTS OF FENG SHUI
BLACK SECT FENG SHUI TRADITION
AN INTRODUCTION TO FENG SHUI PHILOSOPHY
TOOLS OF TRANSFORMATION AND DEVELOPMENT

# I

## INTRODUCTION TO FENG SHUI

## THE ROOTS OF FENG SHUI

### GEOMANCY

All traditional cultures have their own systems of geomancy. Feng Shui is the Chinese interpretation of geomancy. The term geomancy combines the Greek words *Gaea*, meaning "the Mother Earth" and *manteia*, meaning "a system of divination or knowledge." Geomancy is, therefore, a way of knowing the earth. The word first entered the English language in about 1569 first referred to particular forms of divination, and its meaning broadened to include special forms of skillfulness that have to do with uniting people and places in harmony.

For modern society, Feng Shui addresses practical questions—such as where to put a bed or desk or how to site and arrange a home or business—to benefit career, health, marriage, or fame. Both Feng Shui and geomancy can also be used on a larger scale, from community and urban planning to planetary and local healing, balance, and attunement.

In nature, cocoons, webs, nests, dens, and shells attest to the variety and skillfulness of solutions to housing. In these dwellings we can see that an understanding of geomancy is inherent to the survival of a species. The methods employed in a dwelling's construction offer protection from the elements and from predators. (Geomancy is both part of our animal heritage and the result of continuing evolutionary improvement in human society.)

Whatever the level of scientific knowledge or the construction methods employed, people have always developed homes in concert with their environment. Tree houses gave the protection of a nest, while caves could be warmed by fire and offered physical security. Cliff dwellings offered protection from enemies and a view of the surroundings, including visual links to neighboring communities. Sites for Old Stone Age hunting camps were frequently chosen to provide a view, prevent surprise, and give control of an environment. This kind of purposeful planning developed into the "commanding position" principle, a power position to be discussed more fully later.

Geomancy's most basic applications for living are at least a half a million years old, dating from the homosapiens sapiens. From the earliest periods of settled human habitation, we can see practices and methods both of advantageous siting and of methods evoking the Universal Being. For example, early sculptures of the Great Goddess, such as the Venus of Willendorf (right) from 30,000 to 25,000 B.C.E., were placed in interior recesses of homes, not in the vast cave temples of the period, to bring vitality, power, and abundance into people's lives.

FENG SHUI

VENUS OF WILLENDORF

# FENG SHUI

Feng Shui, literally "wind" (*feng*) and "water" (*shui*), is the Chinese name for an intuitive, practical art that seeks to bring people and their environment into the most positive relationship. According to the contemporary definition of Professor Lin, the foremost authority in the world, Feng Shui is the skillful use of the best available knowledge, incorporating both ancient and modern ideas, to create the most suitable conditions for living and working.

The term Feng Shui comes from the following ancient Chinese poem, which describes desirable living conditions:

*The winds are mild.*
*The sun is bright.*
*The water is clear.*
*The trees are lush.*

This poem invokes the image of perfect harmony between Heaven and Earth. Establishing such harmony in our own dwellings will bring positive energy to us. *Chi*, nature's vital energy, can be gathered to bring opportunities, peace, joy, and blessings into our lives.

Feng Shui involves awareness of the many ways housing, location, buildings, and environment can affect a person's daily activities and moods, and influence health, economic life, and relationships. Feng Shui promotes happiness and success by adjusting the interior and surrounding environment of a home or workplace to overcome factors that oppose us and to strengthen what already benefits us.

## KEY MOMENTS IN THE HISTORY OF FENG SHUI KNOWLEDGE

- More than 12,000 years ago, the conditions of the Ice Age led humans to an interiorization of consciousness and inward reflection. This unparalleled development of the psyche's depth is the protohistory of yoga, meditation, and the magical and wisdom arts. People came to better understand the interconnection between self, dwelling, and cosmos.

- Beginning at least 8,000 years ago, shamanism spread vastly. Its key idea of establishing and carefully controlling a proper relationship with nature influenced China's early history. The shaman had the ability to ascend the ridgepole, or World Tree, and thus to journey between Heaven and Earth.

- The growth of cities, based on the idea of the urban center as cosmic center, led to the formal development of the Feng Shui and geomancy systems we have today. While no longer in a rural setting, people still wanted to live in harmony with their surroundings. These systems have a remarkable unity of diversity, meaning that they adapted to different geography by responding with various solutions. They show both unique individuality and tremendous regularity.

Feng Shui was the mother of the natural sciences in China, the original "evironmental impact statement." By knowing the influence of place, weather, cosmos, and all the conditions of our total environment, we can help shape our destiny. For the last 5,000 years, Feng Shui has been used as environmental science, magic, worship, and therapy, to bring security, wealth, harmony, and happiness to homes, communities, workplaces, cities, and countries.

Of the Buddhist schools, the Black Sect, (the tradition I am part of) combines traditional Feng Shui knowledge with the intangible or non-physical concerns, and emphasizes the importance of the user's intention. The Black Sect tradition has helped make Feng Shui a potent force in the West.

Feng Shui uses all available methods in following the *Di Li*, Chinese for "Law of the Earth," to create the best relationships between people and the places they inhabit. Although there are many schools of Feng Shui with important distinctions, all traditions use cosmology, forms, folklore, and other useful knowledge to achieve what is needed.

Professor Lin once commented on the doctrines of Feng Shui schools, stating that if we completely believe what we read in books, it would be better not to read it at all. One book or one doctrine is insufficient. The Yellow River area, where Feng Shui was founded, does not provide all answers, and neither does any one Feng Shui school. Feng Shui has varied from place to place to suit local conditions. However, the principle of using all available knowledge to create the best conditions for living and working remains unchanged.

## FENG SHUI IN THE WORLD TODAY

Feng Shui is practiced openly outside the People's Republic of China, but in China it is forbidden by law, though the law is often unenforced. That does not stop the very people who forbid Feng Shui as superstition in the daytime, however, from seeing a Feng Shui expert for advice at night. China seems to be re-evaluating its standpoint. There is an academic resurgence in studying the Feng Shui heritage of China. China's integration of the city of Hong Kong (which most emphatically uses Feng Shui) may prove an important influence. In coastal Chinese cities Feng Shui is clearly, once again, being used in many projects, indicating an increasing prominence in the thinking of Chinese entrepreneurs and planners. As Feng Shui has gained prominence in the Western world, it has begun to reassert itself in China as well.

## BLACK SECT FENG SHUI

### EVOLUTION OF THE BLACK SECT

The Black Sect teachings of Professor Lin that form the basis of this book are a synthesis of wisdom and shamanic teachings. Its original roots connect it both with Tibetan Buddhism and with the pre-Buddhist Bon religious tradition of Tibet.

When Indian Buddhism entered Tibet in the seventh century, it encountered the pre-existing Bon religion. Buddhist schools in Tibet tried to keep their traditions doctrinally pure. However, the Black Sect took a different approach. It met Indian Buddhism, integrated with it, and developed into something new. The Black Sect was less concerned with doctrinal purity, more open to outside influences. The Indian Tantric Stage can be called the First Stage of Black Sect teaching. The fusion of Indian and Tibetan knowledge in Bon can be called the Second Stage of Black Sect Tantric Buddhism.

Around the year 1100 C.E., the Black Sect moved deeply into China and continued this quality of openness and acceptance. Already a mixture of Tibetan and Indian traditions, the Third Stage of Black Sect tradition encompassed traditional Chinese culture and philosophy, influences from folk religion, Taoism, Confucianism, yin-yang philosophy, *I Ching*, holistic healing methods, normative Chinese Buddhism, eclectic philosophies, and included and emphasized Feng Shui knowledge.

The Fourth Stage of Black Sect Tantric Buddhism began when Professor Lin introduced these teachings to the West. The approach he has taken is apolitical, unorthodox, and nonhierarchical. He reinterpreted Black Sect doctrine and philosophy in terms of modern knowledge, including influences from Western medicine, religion, psychology, social science, architecture, ecology, and natural science as a way to create a bridge between ancient wisdom and modern understanding. His interpretations make Black Sect Feng Shui easy to use, effective to practice, and keep faith with its history and depth.

## THE BLIND MEN AND THE ELEPHANT

The old story of the Blind Men and the Elephant characterizes the special point of view of the Black Sect. In this story, five blind men examine an elephant and each reaches a different conclusion about its nature.

One man, feeling the elephant's trunk, concluded that an elephant must be like a hose. Another, who felt the elephant's leg, decided that an elephant must be like a pillar. A third, feeling the elephant's side, interpreted an elephant as being much like a wall. A fourth blind man examined the elephant's ear and thought an elephant was like a parasol. The fifth, who felt the elephant's tail, decided that an elephant must be like a rope.

Like the five blind men's descriptions of the elephant, people have views of life that vary and are limited. One important tenet of our approach is to respect each point of view. Knowledge that exists today may need to be adjusted in the light of ongoing study as the breadth of knowledge continually expands. What was once secret knowledge, like Feng Shui, becomes public. New knowledge updates old thinking. Black Sect Feng Shui theory has its own view but remains open to and, indeed, tries to make use of all approaches to achieve the greatest good.

## BLACK SECT FENG SHUI TRADITION

Black Sect Feng Shui is the science-art of communication between the *chi*, or life breath, of a place or environment and the *chi* of individuals. Black Sect Feng Shui uses contemporary knowledge mixed with traditional knowledge to find and build the most appropriate places for living and working.

What distinguishes the Black Sect Feng Shui approach from traditional Feng Shui? One important difference is that most traditional schools use the compass and the absolute or cardinal directions as a way of interpreting a given place in terms of wider universal factors. The Black Sect means of doing this involves understanding the site, not in terms of fixed directions or compass positions but in terms of the relative direction from which the *chi* enters and on the site's unique qualities. Where the *chi* comes in is called the *chi kou*, or the "mouth of *chi*." It usually is the main entry, front door, or the primary door of each room. Knowing this, we can superimpose a template on that space and know what area influences which aspect of life.

A second difference between the Black Sect and traditional approaches is that traditional approaches emphasize tangible, objective factors, like the placement of a window, in appraising a location. The Black Sect tends to give a greater emphasis to subjective, intangible forces, derived from one's intuition, while recognizing the great importance of what is seen. Instead of emphasizing the visible and physical, the Black Sect emphasizes the power of body, speech, and mind through the Three Secret Reinforcements, described below.

Traditional Feng Shui methods emphasize physical remodeling or adding physical objects to adjust Feng Shui. If a home is unsuitable, one might be advised to leave. Based on these ideas, a Chinese joke states that if you hire a Feng Shui expert, it is already time to start packing. Conversely, the Black Sect emphasizes ways to remedy problems.

Black Sect Feng Shui emphasizes the importance of meditation and of personal *chi* adjustment to reconcile situations. Some of the most basic and important Black Sect meditative methods, like "calming the heart," "the inhale-exhale" exercise, and "the six–stage *chi* improvement" process, are included in this book.

These methods have a direct relationship to practicing Feng Shui. The unified mind and the increase in intuition they help create allows our Feng Shui eyes to see more clearly.

## THE FACTORS THAT INFLUENCE OUR LIFE CIRCUMSTANCES

Sometimes Feng Shui methods do work like swift miracles, other times only partially, very slowly, or not at all. Sometimes things may even get worse. One reason for imperfect outcomes is that we are subject to many influences. For a situation to improve, all factors that cause the problem, tangible and intangible, personal, family, worldly, mundane, emotional, spiritual, and transcendental should be addressed in the solution.

In life, a large percentage of things do not develop as we would like. If we plant a melon seed, we don't always get a melon. Perhaps we've cared for the melon, watered it, cultivated it, protected it from pests. But just as it ripened, a little boy walking in the garden stepped on it and crushed it. So we do well to accept that all our intentions will not be realized. Professor Lin once remarked that those who want to live a perfect life may come to reside in an insane asylum.

## THE ART OF LIVING

According to traditional Chinese thought, we are subject to many influences. Primary among them are:

- **Fate** (*ming*), or destiny, often understood through astrology—the inheritance and influence of the time and conditions of our birth—is sometimes thought of as immutable. But it can be changed. For example, if we can predict the timing of events, we can adjust for circumstances. Astrology is like a weather report. Knowing it will rain, you can bring an umbrella. If it will be windy, you can wear a windbreaker.

- **Luck** consists of life's variations in fortune, the ups and downs that accompany any life. If we address the factors that control luck, such as fate, Feng Shui, karma, and methods of personal *chi* adjustment, we can change our lives extraordinarily. If we learn to moderate the downs of life and to maximize the ups, we can transform a middling or even a poor fate into a successful life.

- **Feng Shui** is both how the environment conditions us and our influence over our environment.

- **Karma** is the cause and effect of our actions. If we make offerings, and do good deeds, we can adjust karma. A supervening "cause," or a deed we introduce, may have the effect of overcoming a history of negative consequences. People may have the karma to change their karma, to create a "cause" that refreshes.

- **Education,** and the opportunities it creates, also plays an important role in life.

To these influences we may add family circumstances and responsibilities, our place in society, and our ability to give and receive blessings and help.

The Black Sect affirms that Feng Shui can change your destiny. Further, adjusting either luck, karma, or education will affect the other influences. We use the secret, or transcendental, methods of Black Sect Feng Shui and personal *chi* adjustments to change a person, relationship, or environment or to help realize a particular intention.

## ELEMENTAL IDEAS IN FENG SHUI

To understand the methodology of Feng Shui you must be aware of some basic principles.

1. The Earth is alive and has both planetary and local intelligence. Mother Earth is a living being. Feng Shui asserts this idea in many ways that emphasize the interconnected web of life.

2. Wisdom, movement, and energy (connecting *chi* and wisdom): A root concept in Feng Shui is the important connection in ourselves and in our environment of wisdom, movement, and energy. Since ancient times the ideas of blood, water, breath, *chi*, spirit, circulation, machine, organism, and walking have been used to describe movement of the *chi*, or vital energy, of the Earth. One fourteenth-century text refers to a "mysterious network" that "spreads out and joins together every part of the roots of the Earth. . . . Thousands and ten thousands of horizontal and vertical veins like warp and weft weave together in mutual embrace . . . taking all (including Land and Sea) as Earth, the secret and mystery is that the roots communicate with each other."

If the *chi* of the Earth can move through the network, the Earth will be "fragrant and flourishing" and men "pure and wise," but "if stopped up . . . all men and things will be evil and foolish." One of the main goals of Feng Shui is to assure that this energy in our environment is abundant and free in both the interior and exterior of the site.

3. Heaven, human being, and Earth: Another basic idea in Feng Shui is "Heaven, human being, and Earth," which means recognizing the unity and connection of universe, person, and place. Heaven includes cosmological, astrological, calendric, astronomical, or seasonal factors, as well as our sense of structure or intuitively perceived order. Human being is associated with the human body, human culture, human understanding and presence. The Earth is the land itself, its forms, processes, and energies especially this place, your home, your workplace, your town or city.

# AN INTRODUCTION TO FENG SHUI PHILOSOPHY

Learning about the Tao, yin–yang theory, and the importance of *chi* are integral to Feng Shui. To truly know these vital concepts it is not enough just to have an intellectual understanding. You have to see that the Tao (the road of life), yin-yang dualism, and vital energy are in you and in the world and that we function according to the way they operate.

## THE TAI CHI SYMBOL AND YIN–YANG COSMOLOGY

The cosmos consists of both a vast emptiness and at the same time contains all things. The symbol of the cosmos is the tai chi symbol. Tai chi develops from the primordial state, or "great emptiness," as the beginning of all things. It represents, in its original meaning, the "ridgepole" connecting Heaven and Earth in oneness, like the World Tree of shamanism. From the tai chi, yin and yang arise.

Yin (the feminine, passive principle) and yang (the male, active principle) combine in nature to produce all existing relationships. They represent the principle of opposites, the duality that develops from making distinctions such as light and dark, left and right, up and down, front and back, movement and stillness, mountain and valley. Yin and yang express symbolically and metaphorically the qualities, polarities, and transformations of life. For example, the Earth can be seen as yin and the Heavens as yang.

The Earth may be divided into land and water. The moving water is characterized as yang; the land, which usually doesn't move, is yin. On the land we dis-

tinguish dwellings and people. The people, who physically can move, are yang, whereas the places in which they live or work, are considered yin. Among the dwellings we can further distinguish the *yang chai*, the dwellings of the living, and the *yin chai*, the dwellings of the dead, graves and tombs. Among the abodes of the living we can distinguish between homes, which are considered yang because people may be present at any time, and places of work, which are considered yin. Among workplaces, for example, an elementary school, is far more yang than a funeral parlor.

It is important to recognize that the differentiation of yin and yang is not absolute. We can find the yin in the yang, and the yang in the yin. We can continue to make refinements and distinctions, as we understand people and places, and use Feng Shui to balance the yin of an environment with the yang of its inhabitants. One of the things that makes Feng Shui powerful is the yin dimension, or the environment, controls and effects the yang dimension, or the people present in the environment. This gives Feng Shui its ability to create balance, which gives priority to human need by furthering comfort and success over time.

Later we will discuss the Eight Trigrams, the three-line symbols that describe the aspects of life, which we can apply to a plot of land, a home, or a room to know how the trigrams influence our lives. By using these symbols we will see how the tai chi symbol and the yin-yang principle describe in detail the whole world, and in particular our own worlds.

## THE TAO

Without appreciating the Tao, Feng Shui is unfathomable. The word *Tao* (pronounced DOW) means the "way, or path, of life" and is the process in nature

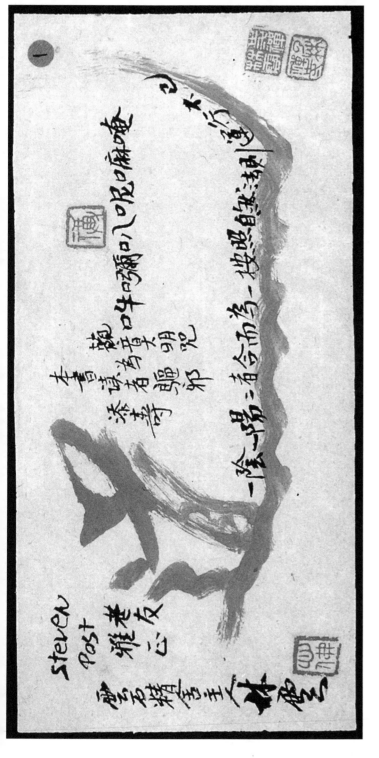

BRUSHSTROKES FOR THE CHINESE CHARACTER OF TAO CAN BE INTERPRETED BY PROFESSOR LIN AS YIN AND YANG TOGETHER FORMING AN ENTITY FOLLOWING NATURE, MOVING ON CEASELESSLY.

by which all things are created, continue, and change. For a life of harmony, this is the path you must take. Applied to the universe, the study of the Tao includes our understanding of cosmology, astronomy, and astrophysics. Applied to the fortunes of nations, studying the Tao includes the study of water and mountains as these influence the fate of nations.

In the Tao of marriage, a man and woman unite and perpetuate themselves into eternity through their children. The Tao of life is expressed as good and bad luck following a pattern creating the ups and downs of life. In Feng Shui, the *chi* of a home and its inhabitants is adjusted to come closer to the harmony and balance of the Tao, and produce beneficial results.

## CHI

The Chinese character for *chi* depicts steam rising over rice (*right*), which provides nourishment. Chi (pronounced CHEE) is considered the life breath that nourishes and vitalizes nature, being, and knowing.

The *chi* of the Earth is of primary importance in Feng Shui. Understanding how to improve the *chi* of our surroundings, ourselves, and of situations is the basic operating principle in Feng Shui.

In our bodies, *chi* is regarded as the true self, or life force, which moves the body, speech, and mind. If the flow of *chi* through the vital organs is smooth, we will have good health. If *chi* does not flow to an arm, it is paralyzed. If *chi* cannot flow to the heart, it will stop and we will cease to live. While the relative state of our *chi* changes continuously as we age and with different experiences, the core of our *chi* remains the same.

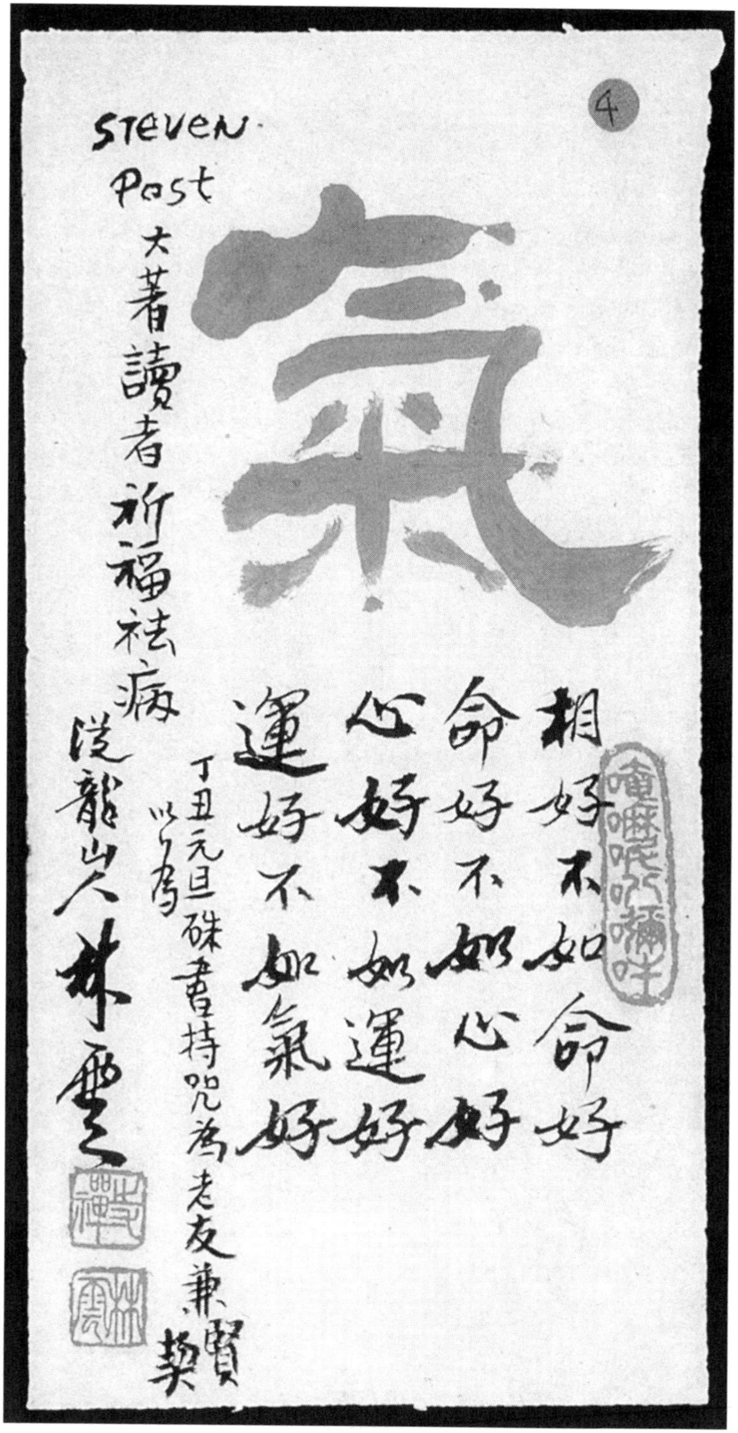

大著讀者　祈福袪病

氣

相好不如命好
命好不如心好
心好不如運好
運好不如氣好

唵嘛呢叭𠺷吽

丁丑元旦殊書持咒為老友兼賢契

沒龍山人　林雲

The Black Sect view of *chi* is very wide ranging. Not only do we consider the flow of *chi* in the Earth or in our bodies but we also consider how *chi* is expressed in a wide variety of situations and personalities. We can speak of the *chi* of the land, the *chi* of the government, or the *chi* of the stock market. The *chi* of Hawaii is not the same as the *chi* of New York City. *Chi* is individual to the geographical area or to the human being it expresses.

We are the primary influence on our own *chi*. Ideally, a person's *chi* is balanced, rising, smooth, and full, filling all of the body and abundant in the head. Some types of *chi* are scholarly, gambling, argumentative, joyous, nosy, wealthy, noble, unlucky, suspicious, rising, depressed, distracted, wicked, and stubborn. *Chi* is also affected by others, by our environment, by events, customs, fads, or by the conduct of people in society.

Respecting and understanding our own *chi* is integral to understanding ourselves. It is in our nature to adjust ourselves. Therefore, if we are exposed to negative *chi* over time, we may adjust ourselves in ways that hurt us.

*Chi* is easy to know because it is the vital force in all things. We can appreciate how our breath is one with the wind and how the wind is one with our breath. To follow the *chi* in nature is in itself therapeutic. If we understand the importance of *chi* in the world, we are easily able to understand the goals of Feng Shui. We can cultivate our own *chi* in many ways, among them:

- Through meditation or Black Sect *chi* adjustment methods (detailed later in this text);

- By either drawing on natural forces or using the spiritual power of a temple, church, sacred site, or natural location;

- By receiving outside help, for example, through a *chi* transfusion from a qualified person;

- With Feng Shui.

(How to analyze the *chi* of the land and how to determine its benefit or harmfulness will be discussed as part of the methods of site analysis presented in this book.)

## TOOLS OF TRANSFORMATION AND DEVELOPMENT

### BASIC BLACK SECT FENG SHUI METHODOLOGY

This book will teach you how to apply Black Sect Feng Shui to your life and your environment. A simplified methodology for doing this has the following four basic points, all of which are detailed below:

1. Memorize the Eight Trigrams (including the Five Element Processes) and build them into your heart;

2. Apply the Eight Trigrams (and Five Elements) to site, home, or room;

3. Use the Three Secret Reinforcements;

4. Use the Method of Minor Additions.

This outlines the basic way to practice Feng Shui and should guide your reading. However, once you are familiar with the principles of Feng Shui and deepen your studies, you can experiment with your own solutions that are not addressed in the book.

## MUNDANE AND TRANSCENDENTAL FENG SHUI SOLUTIONS

In the Feng Shui tradition of the Black Sect of Tibetan Buddhism as taught by Professor Lin, certain combinations of characteristics (form and mind; objective and subjective; visible and invisible; physical and spiritual; mundane and transcendental) are ways of both distinguishing two basic aspects of structure and correcting one's Feng Shui perception and site.

Combining, or "marrying" visible and invisible, tangible and intangible, mundane and transcendental characteristics is the most powerful way to use Feng Shui. Enhancing the relationship between outer and inner forces strengthens Feng Shui actions, connecting spiritual and physical worlds, planes and realms, technique and feeling.

To be completely effective, Feng Shui solutions should use both yin and yang, which together combine to produce all that comes to be. Mundane solutions are yang, which are reasonable, logical, and easily accepted by intellectuals. Transcendental solutions are yin and, although they may seem unreasonable or illogical, we should consider their merit if their results are strong.

For example, if a husband and wife argue, giving them the traditional advice, such as to treat each other like guests, to think before speaking, to think

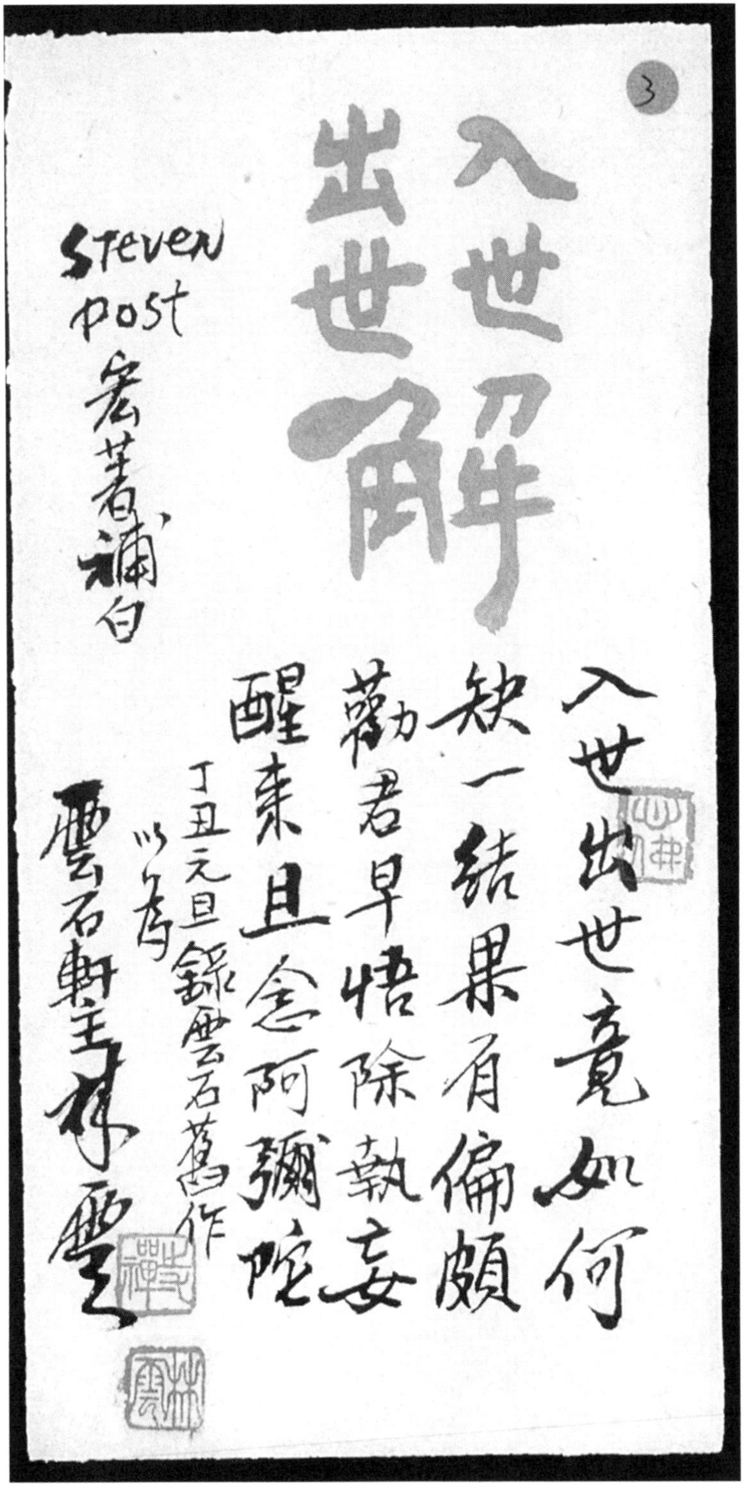

入世
出世

入世
出世一解

STEVEN
POST

名著補白

入世出世竟如何
缺一結果有偏頗
勸君早悟除執妄
醒來且念阿彌陀

丁丑元旦錄雲石舊作
以為

雲石軒主林雲

MUNDANE AND
TRANSCENDENTAL
SOLUTIONS

of themselves as one person, and to avoid mistreating each other, would be considered a mundane solution. Depending on the level of commitment, it might be 5 percent or 10 percent effective.

A more transcendental solution might be to suggest putting a big round mirror on the wall behind their bed and, perhaps, a mirror opposite, on the wall at the foot of their bed, thereby producing an "infinity of mirrors" effect. By adjusting the optic nerves through the sense of space that the mirrors create, this may soften the muscles around the eyes and diffuse a sense of tension that might otherwise erupt into an argument. The greater relaxation of the eyes may correspond to an easier marriage. From a *chi* perspective, we have created a situation where the *chi* can now flow more smoothly, which might be 50 percent effective.

If, however, the couple empowered the mirror using the Three Secret Reinforcements (described later) to express their intention to resolve their problems, the effectiveness of the mirror method might rise from 50 percent to 120 percent. Not only has their problem been solved, but their relationship had been made even better than it was originally.

## THE EIGHT TRIGRAMS

By defining the tai chi symbol, yin–yang cosmology, the Tao, and *chi*, the basis has been established for explaining the Eight Trigrams, which delineate what the parts of your home have to do with your life. After examining how these Eight Trigrams came into being, how they combine in special patterns called *ba kua* (pronounced BAH KWAH) how to overlay this template on a plot, home, or room, we will learn what each trigram area means for us, and how to determine if a given area is missing or enhanced, and what this predicts for a family or individual.

## MANIFESTATION

The Eight Trigrams are an overview and a simplification of all the basic ways the universe manifests itself in our experience. They are the basis for determining the areas of strength and weakness of a site in Black Sect Feng Shui. The trigrams evolved and are comprised from the broken lines that represent yin and the solid lines that represent yang. Each trigram corresponds to a different area in life such as family, career, social life, and mental health. The Eight Trigrams and the tai chi position in the center represent, in symbolic language, the possibilities of creation, the forces that control life, the way things work, and their essential character. Each trigram has the same directional aspect—from top to bottom—that mirrors the flow of *chi*.

The *I Ching*, the ancient Chinese book of philosophy, was developed from the trigrams to explain all of creation as a guide of life. Feng Shui has its intellectual roots in the *I Ching*, and this book is a good place for further study.

## THE BA KUA

The *ba kua*, an arrangement of eight trigrams and a center, serves as a map to match various components of your life with the corresponding areas in your physical world. The Black Sect *ba kua*, or Eight Trigrams, evolved from the Fu Hsi and the King Wen *ba kua*.

# THE FU HSI BA KUA

The traditional story is that Fu Hsi, the first of the Five Legendary Emperors (around 2953–2838 B.C.E.), adopted the symbol of the Earth to represent his reign. He invented the Eight Trigrams by observing the marks on the back of a tortoise. The arrangement, or *ba kua*, he created is called the Former or Early Heaven Sequence or the Abstract or Universal order. It represents the process of creation and dissolution.

# THE KING WEN BA KUA

King Wen (1231–1135 B.C.E.), the founder of the Chou dynasty, was imprisoned for seven years by the Shang tyrant, Emperor Chou Hsin. During his imprisonment he created a new arrangement of the trigrams. This is the Later Heaven Sequence, or temporal order, of the trigrams. It describes in greater detail the functional or phenomenal process of the seasons and of life on Earth, describing how the trigrams function in the world of time.

# BLACK SECT BA KUA

In Black Sect Feng Shui we use a special variation of the King Wen sequence of the trigrams. In this trigram arrangement, we are considered to be standing in the center at the tai chi position.

In the original King Wen version the trigrams move outward from the center. This outward movement reflects the creation of the world and is how karma is created. Our life situations and our actions have effects like a stone thrown in a pool, creating widening concentric circles of outward moving ripples.

Black Sect Feng Shui uses the same King Wen version of the trigrams, but instead of the *chi* moving outward, it moves inward. We are positioned in the center of the trigrams, receiving the *chi* of the trigram flow. Receiving the fruit of your positive karma is implied, transforming the pain of unsatisfactoriness to the fruit of delight, receiving, accepting. Experiencing the trigrams coming toward us in the center, we learn how to understand ourselves as a center, how to be whole. The overlay of the Black Sect *ba kua* on our environment, whether physically on an outline of the site or through visualization, addresses how to take action to transform ourselves with Feng Shui.

Each trigram represents a huge constellation of meanings. I highly recommend that you learn each trigram by its Chinese name and learn to associate each trigram with the numerous attributes associated with it, including color, compass direction, areas of the body, and family members. By avoiding thinking of the trigrams with English keywords, you will not unconciously link each trigram to a single concept, like "wealth" or "family" or "marriage." Instead you will be able to apply the most important meaning as needed for the situation.

The Eight Trigrams show a deep appreciation of yin and yang. It should be the goal of a person who wants to use the trigrams skillfully to know them almost as you know a close friend, to relate to the trigrams personally and intimately in terms of feeling and energy. We also need to know how to relate the trigrams with each other. We will use these trigrams in the Black Sect *ba kua* to uncover the strengths and weaknesses of a room, building, or site.

# THE MEANINGS OF THE TRIGRAMS

Discussing the basic meanings of the trigrams could fill a book. Each trigram has at least fifty basic associations that could be important in a given Feng Shui case. The most basic and important meanings for Feng Shui: life category, color, element, position in the family, direction, and body part, are listed in the chart, opposite. Further explanations of the trigrams follow:

- **Chen** (pronounced JEN), according to the Wood element, is like a blade of grass that pushes the Earth aside, representing the ability to initiate things and make new beginnings. It also represents family.

- **Hsun** (pronounced SHUN), sharing the Wood element association, is like a fully grown, mature tree, representing the ability to fully open to abundance, and wealth.

- **Li** (pronounced LEE) has to do with seeing and being seen, rank, reputation, recognition, status and place in society.

- **Kun** (pronounced KUN), has to do with the Earth who cares for and nourishes all things. It has to do with relationships and partnerships in the sense of both marriage and business, and with women.

- **Tui** (pronounced D'WAY) has to do with completing things fully and with joy, like a successful harvest. It represents our descendants and in that sense, our future plans and projects.

- **Chyan** (pronounce CHYAN) is refined metal, like a tool or sword. This

# BLACK SECT BA KUA

trigram represents benefactors or with receiving timely help. In this way it is associated with Heaven and men.

- **Kan** (pronounced KHAN) represents our ancestral foundation. Through its association with water, kan has to do with our ability to reflect a situation without imposition or prejudice, to exercise judgment, cognitive ability, and learning ability. Through its association with moving water, *kan* has to do with the social context, the ocean of people in which we swim. Thus it has to do with career and with social life.

- **Ken** (pronounced GEN) has to do with skillfulness, the way we handle things. It includes academic ability, self-knowledge, and also self-cultivation and the impulse to enlightenment.

The tai chi position in the center of the chart oversees all areas not covered by the trigrams, especially with physical and mental health. It also can be used for family members or parts of the body not detailed in the Eight Trigrams. It is associated with the Earth as well and with the colors brown and yellow.

# USING THE EIGHT TRIGRAMS

## IN FENG SHUI

When we superimpose the trigrams on a given area, literally or figuratively, we understand that the trigrams completely cover the given plot or boundary of a site, house, room, bed, face, or geographic area, like the squares of a tic-tac-toe board. According to the shape of the plot, house, or room, one or more trigrams may be missing or strengthened. If, for example, you were making an adjustment for wealth, which corresponds to the *hsun* position, you might place a windmill in the *hsun* position on your site. Place green plants in the *hsun* position of your house. Put a fish tank in the *hsun* position of your living room, and use other secret methods in other *hsun* positions of your home. By energizing multiple areas, you help achieve the most effective result.

In understanding a site and applying the *ba kua*, Black Sect Feng Shui is flexible about the overlay of the trigrams. We apply the *ba kua* to the site based, not on the fixed compass directions of other Feng Shui schools, but on where you determine the "mouth of *chi*" is in your site, building, or room.

The mouth of *chi* is where the *chi* comes into a room, a home, a plot, city, or geographic region. In our homes and workplaces, the front door and the primary entryways into each room are the mouths of *chi*. It is the guide for overlaying the Eight Trigrams on the area to determine the strengths and weaknesses of that area. Identifying the mouth of *chi* can be applied at many levels of scale, including regions where highways and airports could be the main mouth of *chi*, neighborhoods, driveway entrances, and the front doors of our homes.

# THE THREE-DOOR BA KUA METHOD

How to overlay the trigrams on a house or room is accomplished with the three-door *ba kua* method as follows:

1. Find the mouth of *chi*. Imagine you are standing in the doorway looking inward.

2. Determine the *kan wall* or *line*. This is the line where *ken*, *kan*, and *chyan* are aligned.

3. Determine the trigram that corresponds to the door.

4. Overlay the Eight Trigrams on the site.

A Feng Shui student must build the arrangement into his heart. By memorizing the Black Sect Trigram pattern and learning to use it, you will always carry this knowledge within you so that you can apply it anywhere. Once you know how to determine the mouth of *chi*, apply the *ba kua*, or arrangement, automatically on a location, the position of the trigrams will allow you to determine the quality of each position and accordingly apply techniques found in this book to improve the situation.

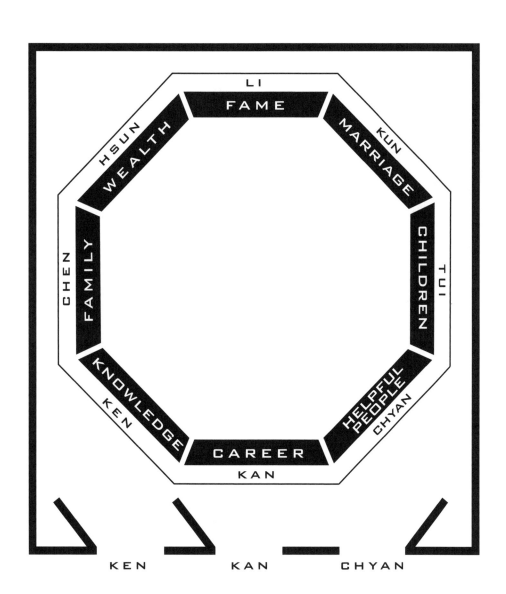

## FINDING THE MOUTH OF CHI

If two doors are used equally, determine which is the primary door. Perhaps one is used more. The critical route or major path leading to a building, apartment, or room is important. Observe how people come in. The first door they meet will determine which door to use as the mouth of *chi*. If the door is slanted, the determination of its trigram position is dependent on how people primarily enter. If as you face the door from the outside people come from the left, the door is a *chyan* door. If people come from the right, it is a *ken* door.

Pay attention to pedestrian and automobile traffic. For a corner door on a busy street, the preponderance of traffic gives the key to whether the door is *chyan* or *ken* and how the trigrams will be overlaid on that store or building. For the second story of a site, determine the mouth of *chi* for that floor and overlay the trigrams accordingly.

## THE EVER-CHANGING EIGHT TRIGRAMS

The phrase "ever-changing Eight Trigrams" means that how the trigrams are applied with the three-door *ba kua* method changes depending on the location of the mouth of *chi* of the room, building, or site. The *ba kua*, or pattern, rotates or changes so that the *ken-kan-chyan* trigrams are placed along the same line as the mouth of *chi*. The overlay on a site, building, or room can be either physical, by using a blueprint or diagram, or mental, by envisioning the area as a flat plane. A plot of land will have the *ba kua* overlaid based on its entry road. A house will have a *ba kua* overlaid based on its door. A room will have the *ba kua* overlaid based on its main door. The *ba kua* can also be applied to the bed or to the face or hands.

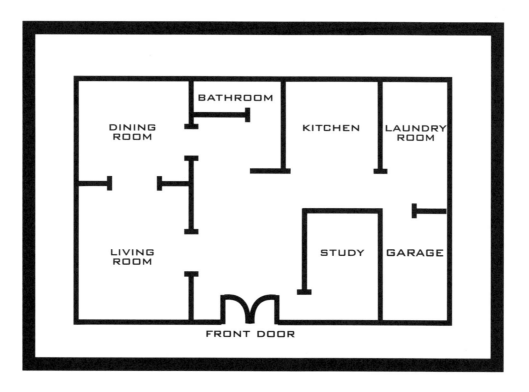

To review, we have seen how the trigrams are generated and how they have qualities, energies, and meaning. We've learned to overlay the Black Sect *ba kua* on a plot, house, or room. Now it's time to play "Name That *Kua!*"

Once you have determined the way the *ba kua* should be overlaid, notice in your home or workplace each room in terms of the *ba kua* and see what is strong, weak, or missing. Investigate needs in your own life to issues in that environment.

A

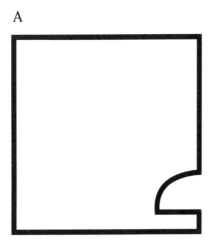

In case A, the door is at the left. The door is connected to which trigram? (Answer: *ken.*)

B

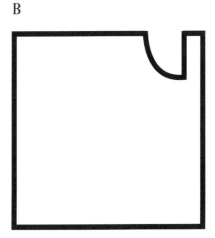

In case B? (Answer: *ken.*)

C

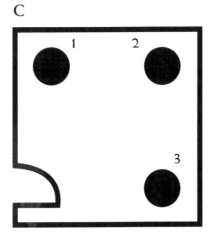

In case C? (Answer: *chyan.*)
In case C, what trigrams are in positons 1, 2, and 3?
(Answer: *ken, hsun,* and *kun.*)

D

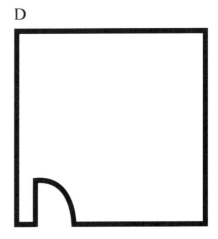

Finally, in case D, what trigram is the door associated with? (Answer: *ken.*)

## How to Know if an Area Is Missing or Enhanced
### When You Overlay the *Ba Kua*

Almost always, a *ba kua* analysis based on the mouth of *chi* and the three-door *ba kua* method is accurate. However, how to overlay the *ba kua* on a room is subject to interpretation. If you have a shape that is not rectangular, the basic rule for knowing if something is missing or strengthened is as follows:

## STRENGTHENING BA KUA
## PROJECTIONS

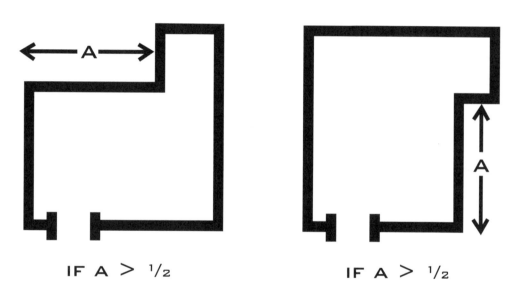

IF A > ¹/₂              IF A > ¹/₂

If *A is greater than half either* vertically or horizontally, we have a strengthening projection. In the example given, the *kun* trigram is a projection strengthening the areas of life connected with *kun* (marriage, woman, mother, stomach, etc.).

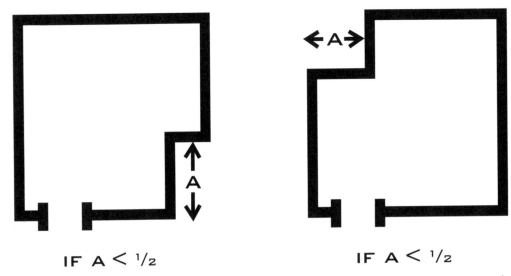

**IF A < ½**   **IF A < ½**

If A is less that 1/2 either vertically or horizontally we have an area with a missing trigram.

If you have a case where the distances are equal you can use your intuition to feel if something is missing. Generally, it is wise to correct a possibly missing area using the Method of Minor Additions, described later in the book.

Practice overlaying the Eight Trigram template on homes, rooms, plots of land, and public places. Combine this study with self-cultivation in meditation and personal *chi* adjustment described later in the text so that your intuition and technical knowledge grow together.

# THE FIVE ELEMENT PROCESSES

The Five Element Processes are absolutely basic to Feng Shui understanding, because how the Five Elements function as agents of change stimulates and shapes our daily lives. The Chinese Five Elements (Metal, Water, Wood, Fire, and Earth) represent the functional situation of life on this planet, the way things come into being, increase and decrease, are generated or overcome. There is a natural order or sequence to these elements, which, when used properly, can help develop harmony, prosperity, and happiness.

Each element has its own qualities and significance, which can be applied in Feng Shui to forms, such as house or hill shapes, to social psychology, such as understanding another's *chi*, and to balancing one's own personal *chi*. Aligning the Five Elements and the Eight trigrams is basic in Feng Shui.

The primal *chi* as represented by the tai chi symbol in the Black Sect *ba kua* manifests itself in the Five Elements. The basis of the Eight Trigrams are four phases, which correspond to the four seasons of the year; the fifth element, Earth, is thought of as being the center.

While some Chinese traditions hold that a person has one basic ruling element, Black Sect Feng Shui theory believes that each of us has the *chi* of all the Five Elements. We need to balance and adjust the elements in our personal *chi*, not to even everything out but so we are dynamically balanced in a way that respects our unique individuality.

When we consider the behavior of other people in terms of the Five Elements, remember that the descriptions are simplifications and apply in very situational ways. A person may be social in one context and withdrawn in another. We may be reliable sometimes but not always. In investigating the way people act and interact or in negotiating with others, we can use the "production order" and "overcoming order" element sequences (described later) to our advantage.

When applying the Five Elements to forms, you can determine the overall characteristic of a body of water or a building based on its corresponding hill element shape.

## METAL

The rounded hill is the Metal type, the prototype of the earliest kind of mine where an exposed vein of ore could easily be accessed. It is also the tree shape.

Metal is contracting, heavy, inward moving, cold, and stagnant. It is connected with the west and autumn, the color white, the lungs and large intestine, a pungent taste, and the sound of weeping. A maximum amount of the *chi* of Metal will make an individual talkative, demonstrative, nosy, enthusiastic, and possibly self-righteous. Someone with more balanced *chi* of Metal speaks up appropriately against injustice. She expresses herself well. If it is correct, this kind of person can hold her tongue. Someone with a very low amount of Metal may be withdrawn, shy, speaking little, having choked *chi*. These people may have their own opinions and tend to keep it to themselves. The virtue of Metal is righteousness.

# WATER

The rippling or meandering hill and weeping tree shapes are the Water types.

Water is fluid, liquid, downward moving, cool, and gentle. It is connected with the north and with winter, the kidneys and bladder, a salty taste, and the sound of groaning. The virtue associated with the Water element is wisdom. The *chi* of water has two aspects in terms of character: still water and moving, or dynamic, water.

Still water represents intellectual capacity and wisdom, cognitive and learning ability, clarity, and judgment. A maximum amount of still water would be like an ocean of infinite wisdom. Still water *chi* is described in terms of natural features. It includes a lake (a person of broad knowledge), a pool (a person of narrow knowledge), a creek, a mud puddle, and an old well.

Moving water has to do with movement in terms of social activities or career. Someone with high moving water is like an ocean, traveling without boundaries, with strong *chi* moving brain and body. Such a person is often not at home. A great lake represents less movement. A big river, movement in one direction; a spring or a fountain, a personality that repeats itself or is very routinized, going from work, to the same supermarket and then home, for example. Moving water has to do with the social context, the ocean of people in which we swim. It has to do with career, business, and social life. Moving water also has to do with cash flow.

# WOOD

The columnar hill and oval tree shapes are the Wood types.

Wood is expansive, creative, upward, consuming yet creating as it does so, sprouting. It is connected with the east and with spring and the world of nature. It is associated with the liver and gallbladder, a sour taste, and the sound of shouting. The *chi* of Wood spans a continuum between being opinionated and having no opinion. Persons with a high degree of the *chi* of Wood are designated "betel palm" or "bamboo" *chi* types. These personalities are stubborn, inflexible, prejudging, and tend not to be able to hear other's ideas. Someone with more balanced *chi* of Wood is called the "big tree" type. They can listen and evaluate, think before accepting a point of view, and change their minds if appropriate. A low degree of Wood *chi* is called the "duck weed" or "floating weed" type. This kind of person has no strong opinions or no opinion at all, easily going along with what is presented, like a floating weed on a lake blown by the wind.

The virtue associated with the Wood element is human heartedness. It refers to benevolence, kindness, love, and extending to the world the feeling you have for those with whom you are intimate.

## FIRE

The pointed or triangular hill or mountain and pyramidal shape tree are the Fire types, whose prototype is a volcano before it blows its top. Sharp zigs and zags, and pointed water formations also represent fire.

Fire is explosive, hot, consuming, destroying, speeding up, moving upward. It is connected with the south and with summer. It is related to the heart, the small intestines, and the eyes. Its taste is bitter. Its sound is laughter. Its characterological expression has to do with anger. Typically, anger may be aroused by a sense that something is unreasonable or that our power is being taken away. A person with a high degree of the *chi* of Fire is easily aroused to anger. Such a person may make trouble or have an explosive personality. A person with more balanced *chi* of Fire is more reasonable and appropriate. Two types of a low amount of the *chi* of Fire should be mentioned. In one, a person facing inequality, social pressure, or the attacks of others is unable to express anger. This can easily come to cause internal illnesses, such as heart disease or ulcers. Another low *chi* of Fire type actually is able to completely swallow Fire *chi*, processing it completely and remaining uninjured. The virtue of Fire is propriety, etiquette, decorum, and reasonable behavior.

## EARTH

The rectangular or square hill and a vase tree shape are connected with the Earth Element. A right angle in a stream associates it with Earth.

Earth is stable, harmonious, firm but not rigid, reliable, still but not stagnant. It is in some ways the most complex of the elements. The most important element to adjust, it is connected with the central position. It is related to the spleen and the stomach. Its taste is sweet. It is the sound of singing. Earth element *chi* ranges from selfishness to selflessness, from egocentrism to generosity. It has to do with how we take care of ourselves and others. It has to do with making boundaries and how we give and receive.

Persons with a high degree of Earth *chi* will tend to sacrifice themselves for others. They have the "spirit of the match." They may burn themselves up for others. If I approach a person with excessive Earth *chi* and ask to borrow money to take some friends to dinner, the high Earth *chi* individual may give me his last dollar and even go hungry. Someone with more balanced *chi* of Earth cares both for himself and for others, in this way, avoiding the danger of burnout. Such a person can say no and not feel badly about it. On the other hand, those with a very low amount of *chi* of Earth tend to be quite selfish. They look to their own advantage and use others to help their own cause.

The virtue of Earth is trustworthiness, reliability, faithfulness.

## Element Orders and Feng Shui

The elements have a few natural orders or sequences. For basic Feng Shui use, the two most important are the "production or generating order" of the elements and the "overcoming or destructive order" of the elements. Both the productive and the overcoming sequences of the elements can be used positively in Feng Shui.

## THE PRODUCTION ORDER

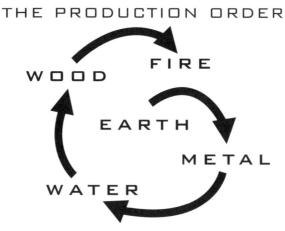

In the production or generating order:

Water produces Wood.
Wood produces Fire.
Fire produces Earth.
Earth produces Metal.
Metal produces Water.

(This sequence should be memorized.)

The production order describes natural events. It rains and the hills turn green; plants need water to grow. Wood can be burned by fire; if we add wood to the stove, the fire grows. As the fuel of fire, wood can be seen as its productive agent. Fire produces earth; wood burned becomes ashes like earth. Earth produces metal; minerals have been thought of as growing in the earth. They are the Earth's constituents or productions. Metal "produces" water; metal can sweat or, when heated, become liquefied, taking on a watery state.

## THE OVERCOMING ORDER

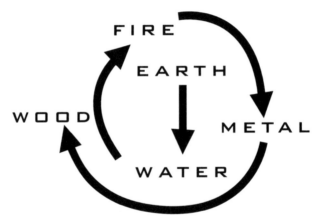

In the overcoming or destructive order:

Earth overcomes Water.
Water overcomes Fire.
Fire overcomes Metal.
Metal overcomes Wood.
Wood overcomes Earth.

(This sequence should be memorized.)

When water floods from levees to sandbags, earth is used to stem the flood. Water puts fire out. Fire melts metal. Metal (an ax) chops wood. Wood pushes earth aside, as a blade of grass bursts through the ground or a tree disrupts the foundation of a house.

## USING THE FIVE ELEMENTS IN FENG SHUI

Consider the relationship among the elements. Learn to distinguish the elements in terms of color, shape, and materials. Apply this knowledge to distinguish the element activity at a site, among a group of homes, or in relationships within a neighborhood, a site, or a house.

For example, you can use a Five Element color corresponding to a trigram position to correct a problem connected with that position. If you are having a problem involving the flow of people in your life, such as moving to a new town or seeking a new job, you can add black (the color for the element Water) to the *kan* position of your home, which deals with social life.

### ELEMENT COLORS

You can use the colors associated with the elements in a production or overcoming order for interiors or exteriors in Feng Shui:

Water: black
Wood: green or blue
Fire: red
Earth: yellow or brown
Metal: white

So using the orders we learned earlier, in the production order:

| Black | Green | Red | Yellow | White |
|---|---|---|---|---|
| generates | generates | generates | generates | generates |
| green | red | yellow | white | black |

In the overcoming order:

| Black | Red | White | Green | Yellow |
|---|---|---|---|---|
| overcomes | overcomes | overcomes | overcomes | overcomes |
| red | white | green | yellow | black |

Black Sect color theory holds that you should not avoid any colors, but you may address problems by using the colors of the Five Elements. You can interpret the colors very generally. For example, red means the whole family of red. You can choose pastels or special families of color.

Generally speaking, when using the elements to strengthen an area of your life, you can use the production order to get quick results and strong development, and the overcoming order for results that are very enduring and potent. Whether you use the production sequence or the overcoming sequence, the key is the flow you create. Examples of how to create different types of flow follow; be sensitive to match it to the environment and to the need. (Five Element color theory is also discussed in the Method of Minor Additions)

# EXTERIORS AND INTERIORS

In exterior or interior design, you may use the colors of the elements in either the productive or destructive cycles and use these sequences both from top to bottom and from bottom to top. Either way will generate a positive result.

For an exterior, if you notice that the buildings around you are brown or yellow, you might use the production order and paint your house white, with black trim. In this way you are saying, in color language, yellow (Earth) produces white (Metal) which produces Black (Water). Use at least three of the element colors to create a sequence. If in the example above, you added some green trees with red flowers or made the roof green with a red weather vane you are using all the Five Elements, which provides a special sense of completeness. This complete Five Element method can also be used within a home for the interior of a room.

You may use the production cycle, for example, in having a green carpeted floor, pale pink walls, and a ceiling with a yellow tint. You may add some white shaded lamps with black stands to incorporate all the Five Elements.

## The Intention of Your Home and the Use of the Will

The role of intention and imagination is emphasized in the Three Secret Reinforcements of Black Sect Feng Shui. Worldwide, geomancy has always emphasized the "concurrence of outward form and inner purpose," which means reinforcing the adjustments in the physical world with your personal desire to make that change. The integration of mundane and transcendent, outer and inner, form and mind, characterizes successful Feng Shui.

## THE THREE SECRET REINFORCEMENTS

The Three Secret Reinforcements are the Black Sect way to use the three aspects of a human being—body, speech, and mind—to express intention and will to empower a Feng Shui action, a meditation method, or a personal *chi* adjustment. Physical or mundane acts, such as hanging mirrors or plants or moving a bed or desk, are combined with the use of intention, which we express with our body, our speech, and our mind to bring the completeness of our being to the act. It is a Black Sect Tantric Buddhist practice, but it can be used with any system of belief.

Using the Three Secret Reinforcements, we discover how to prepare our minds to receive what we want, and we learn how better to link our own desire with "the impulse to enlightenment." Using the Three Secret Reinforcements to empower a Feng Shui installation or solution or a personal *chi* adjustment involves:

- **Body**: Use hand gesture (mudra) to express the power of the body.

- **Speech**: Use mantra, prayer, or affirmation.

- **Mind**: Visualize and intend the desired result.

Let us say that you have put up a mirror, moved your bed, or hung a crystal ball for Feng Shui purposes. Having completed this physical action, employ the Three Secret Reinforcements to seal that action with intent.

## BODY

The mudra, or gesture, is an expression with the hands to remove obstacles and to affirm what we wish. Generally, we use the dispelling evil mudra, also called the ousting or subjugating mudra, which is sometimes employed to place a curse. (In Black Sect tradition it is never used this way. If you use these methods to do harm, it is extremely dangerous for you.) We use the mudra to send negativity away.

Generally, men use the left hand while women use the right hand to form and use this mudra. (See photos.) The two middle fingers (the middle and ring fingers) are bent and the thumb is placed on their fingernails. The pointer and pinkie are extended. Flick the middle fingers outward. One flick is one repetition of the dispelling evil mudra. You not only expel the bad, or remove the blockage, but retain the auspicious and positive *chi*. You may visualize God's light or Buddha's light coming out of your fingers, destroying all obstacles and driving out all evil.

# SPEECH

The "speech secret" is mantra or prayer. In Black Sect tradition we most often use *Om Ma Ni Pad Me Hum* as our speech secret (pronounced OHM MAH KNEE PAD ME HUNG). This mantra invokes the power of universal compassion and accomplishment. The mantra of Tonpa Shenrab Miwoche, the Black Sect Buddha and his consort the Great Goddess of Wisdom Sherab Jyamma, can also be used. It is *Om Ma Tri Mu Ye Sa Le Du* (pronounced OHM MAH TREE MOO YEH SAH LAY DOO). This mantra represents in the sequence of its syllables the Buddha, his consort, and his six manifestations who enlighten each realm of existence.

It is Black Sect doctrine to fully respect individual belief and to apply the Three Secret Reinforcements in an appropriate way for each person. The speech secret you use should invoke compassion and universal support. For Roman Catholics the Litany of the Blessed Virgin is very good. The Our Father (and also the corresponding esoteric Our Mother prayer) may be excellent for other Christians. The *Shema*, including the initial *Ail Melech Neheman* (God is a true king) is appropriate for Jews, as is the *Shema Kolenu* section of the *Amida*. *La Ilah Il Allah Hu* or *Allahu Akbar* can be used by Moslems. An atheist may express the supporting power of the universe audibly by making a verbal affirmation of choice, such as "The Universe will assist and support me in achieving my purpose."

# MIND

The mind secret involves visualizing the desired result, the purpose connected with positioning an object or adjusting personal *chi*. You visualize what you want to happen.

Understand that we get not only what we think but what we feel. Therefore, it is very important to have a positive feeling as you visualize achieving the desired result. Be happy, as if you have already received what you desire. It is significant also to feel the importance of getting what you want.

Visualize the result happening step by step. You can visualize the beginning, successful middle, and completely realized conclusion, or create a mental scenario of nine segments in which your purpose is fully realized. Nine is the most yang, or active of numbers for repetitive sequences. For example, in buying a house, you can see yourself coming upon an excellent building and noticing it as a possible home, contacting your agent, touring the building, returning for a second look with your family, making an offer, hearing a counteroffer, coming to terms, going through escrow and closing, then happily moving in. (Sometimes the reasons blocking us from achieving our purpose are revealed in the process.) Notice any resistence or "counter-intention" you may have to achieving the outcome you want.

Repeat this process of using body, speech, and mind nine times to fully empower a Feng Shui object or method. If you make any Feng Shui adjustments without the Three Secret Reinforcements, they will still have some desired effect. But the effectiveness of these methods will be greatly optimized if you use the Three Secrets.

## THE METHOD OF MINOR ADDITIONS

The Method of Minor Additions, *Xie Zi Fa* (pronounced SHYEH TZI FAH), is the technique of adding an object to adjust the flow of *chi* in a site. The principle is very simple. In a missing area or an area to be enhanced, place something that will adjust the *chi* appropriately. While the principle of 4 ounces (the minor addition) overcoming 800 pounds (the bad influence) is connected with the martial arts, its roots are in Feng Shui. The essence of this "small conquering large" methodology is how to use a little bit to achieve a great deal. For example, a spotlight may overcome the influence of a steep slope. A mirror may open a hundred doors. The strength of the minor addition is reinforced by making use of the Three Secret Reinforcements.

The methods outlined below are just a guide and can be applied in many ways. The uses of objects presented are fundamental. You might come up with a cure more suitable for your unique situation. The category "others," in almost every appearance on the Black Sect Feng Shui overview chart, is considered, potentially, to be the most important. So use this category in keeping with your own creativity and style.

## BRIGHTNESS AND ADDING BRIGHT OBJECTS

### CRYSTALS

Multifaceted spherical crystals are used to adjust the direction of *chi* flow. The crystal ball takes a linear flow and diffuses it in all directions. When the *ling* or the bad karma or the difficult *chi* hits a crystal ball, you never know that the bad influence has come in or that it has been corrected. Crystals can help improve the effectiveness of your visualization by reflecting spiritual light, sunlight, the light of the deity of your own heart, or simply universal light. Often you may substitute a mirror or a wind chime for a crystal. Place crystals in places like hallways or along the alignment of three or more "piercing heart doors," as well as, above where you sit or in a place of negative impact, such as between a door to a bathroom and your bed. Also a crystal ball (hung from the rearview mirror) in your car can be empowered for safety and calmness.

# LIGHTS

This class of cures involves the sense of sight. Lights are among the most powerful Feng Shui tools, because vision is fundamental to sensory experience. In general, you can improve an environment by brightening it. Generally, in using lights, their potential illumination is much more important than their actual illumination. Whether you shine one or nine spotlights at your roof to adjust for a missing *hsun* position, the light doesn't need to be on all the time; a few hours at night is enough.

## EXTERNAL LIGHTING

Ground lighting, such as spotlighting the roof or the area above the front door can be an effective way to raise the *chi* of a house. Spotlights on the roof aimed up toward a central apex is also a potent method to lift the *chi* of a home.

Lights can be added to the plot of your house to balance the plot shape. Or, if your house is below the level of the road, a spotlight beamed back from the downslope side to the highest part of the building will lift the *chi*. If lighting is impossible, you could use three large flagpoles or plant nine bamboo trees instead. For a "dustbin-shaped house" you may spotlight either the front of the house or the back to increase the possibility of receiving good things.

You can balance a house with a spotlight above the front door. Lights on either side of a front door can be like guardians. Motion-sensor lights, which are increasingly prominent in lighting exteriors, can also be used with great effectiveness to increase the visibility of an area indoors.

## INTERNAL LIGHTING

A bright light that turns on automatically as you enter an area that has limited visibility encourages cogent thinking. The bright light also creates a feeling of space.

## MIRRORS

Mirrors have been called the "aspirin of Feng Shui." My associate, Barry Gordon, and I joke that if someone calls us late at night with a Feng Shui problem we may advise the caller to: "Take two mirrors and call us in the morning!" Mirrors control, create space, counteract negative factors, and allow good things—like a beautiful view—to enter.

Mirrors can benefit an area in the following ways:

1. Counteract or cancel out a bad influence. If as you enter a home there is a feeling of pressure, close quarters, or darkness, a mirror on the wall facing the entrance can alleviate and remove the difficult influence. Or if a roof ridge points at your bedroom, a mirror on an exterior wall on the outside of the house, empowered by the Three Secret Reinforcements, can counteract the negative impact of the pointed energy, neutralizing the effect.

2. Eliminate bad *chi*. Mirrors can alter *chi* by increasing the domain of vision, drawing attention to ourselves, directing our *chi* to the mirror to enhance it, or making a sharp point, which focuses bad *chi* our way, disappear from view.

3. Attract or bring in auspicious *chi*. Mirrors can be used to attach, attract, or pull in a positive energy from outside the home. On a wall opposite a view of natural beauty, place a mirror. What you see in the mirror will be the beautiful scene. Attaching a beautiful ocean view in your line of site may enhance your ability to think or write. If you can't see the street from your front door, mirrors can disclose that view from a window and allow you to avoid missing opportunities.

4. Enable the *chi* to flow. If you have a door that is never opened, or one you have deliberately blocked, it is called a "dead door." Perhaps in a room with four doors you would like to seal off two of them. Placing a mirror on such doors will allow the *chi* to flow through and not be blocked. Mirrors in this way can prevent stagnant *chi* and allow *chi* to circulate smoothly. Even a relatively small mirror will negate the bad feeling of stuck *chi*.

5. Dissect. Sometimes mirrors can split the visual aspect of a bad situation, such as a tree too close to the entrance of your home, creating a dissipating effect. If a large nearby building is broken visually into two or more images in a mirror, the influence of its oppressive negative *chi* is substantially reduced.

6. Expand. Mirrors create a feeling of space. For this reason, if a mirror is placed on a wall where a trigram area is missing, it can have the effect of filling in what is missing and thus complete and expand that space.

7. Turn an image upside down. Turning an image upside down is a way of minimizing its force. A convex mirror can be used to reduce the feel-

ing of pressure of a larger building or threatening visual impact. If tall buildings loom on your left and right, creating the feeling of being in a valley, turning the image of the buildings on either side upside down symbolically reduces their influence.

8. Reflect. If the *chi* is directed too strongly at your house, such as when the leg of a T-intersection aims at your house or a road approaches you like an arrow or a small gap between two buildings aligns with your home or the roof ridge or the side of a building is aimed at you, a mirror can reflect the influence. You can hang a *ba kua* mirror, a mirror surrounded with the *fu hsi* trigram sequence, outside the home facing the linear impact to be reflected.

Alternatively, a *ba kua* mirror can be hung upside down on an interior wall, so the *chyan* trigram is at the bottom. Empower the mirror to act like a sword, cutting and overcoming the negative influence.

9. Reject. If a sharp force or other problematic influence is seen in the mirror, the mirror can overcome that kind of influence by rejecting or dismissing it.

10. Strengthen. For example, when people ring the doorbell, if you can look downward from an upper floor and see in a mirror who is there, a mirror has been used to strengthen you by increasing your viewing area.

11. Show movement. The effect of reflecting moving shadows brings the natural cycle of the day into the home. It is a way of invigorating an interior by engaging the sun's movement and reflecting into the home

the variations of clouds, wind blowing trees, moonlight, or other natural forces.

12. Others. In Black Sect Feng Shui mirrors are not avoided in the bedroom. A large round mirror behind the master bed can relax the eyes, diffuse tension, and help improve the marriage. Combined with a mirror near the foot of the bed, an infinite doubling of the mirror image can instill a feeling of joyful expansion, completion, and advancement. Mirrors can also be placed to the left and right of a bed. This same principle can also be used in the office.

A small round one-sided mirror can be affixed to the ceiling above where you sit or lie to lift your *chi* upward, invigorating mental processes. A similar mirror could be placed on the ceiling over a toilet, if the toilet is in a problematic trigram position, like in the *hsun* position or in the center of the house, and can be empowered to help keep your wealth from being flushed away.

## MIRROR FENG SHUI FOR BABIES

Mirrors enhance development. After the period of extreme nearsightedness, infants, helped by mirrors, develop more rapidly, expanding their horizons and increasing both socialization and integration with the world. Infants are fixated on the face; it is their first experience of associating themselves and the world. Note how a newborn will respond to seeing tongue movement by moving its own tongue.

# Sound

Using the sense of hearing can be powerful in Feng Shui. Adding a pleasant sound can adjust many Feng Shui situations.

## WIND CHIMES

A wind chime can be used, much like a crystal, to radiate sound in an omnipresent way. In doing so it can adjust the direction of the flow of *chi* by diffusing and radiating a linear impact like that of a road, hallway, or staircase facing the front door, diverting the *chi* and relieving pressure. The wind chime's tubes should be of metal and produce a clean, sweet, clear sound. It is desirable for the wind chime to have five ringing tubes, which would represent the combined power of the Five Element Processes. A wind chime can:

- Call attention to the gifts you have to offer the world and can help promote career, fame, and prosperity.

- Alert, awaken and clear one's mind. Chimes can also increase a person's intellect.

- Draw attention and make an impression.

- Uplift one's *chi*. If someone spends an inordinate amount of time in bed, place a wind chime in the center of the bedroom. This method is used if someone is depressed, lazy, can't achieve anything, or is suicidal.

- Adjust direction of *chi* flow.

- Improve one's fame or reputation.

- Make transcendental solutions, such as the Three Secret Reinforcements, more effective. The Chinese word for wind chime is *feng ling*, or wind bell. But *ling* also sounds exactly like the word for spiritual. So place a wind chime in the area you want to correct with trancendental solutions.

- Others. If you can see the stove from the front door (a *chi* situation that can detrimentally affect a family's health, instigating accidents, violence, and operations), place a wind chime at the front door or over the stove where the cook stands or between the door and the stove.

## BELLS

Bells can be used as a warning. A shopkeeper's bell on a front door allows residents to keep tabs on who may be entering. Bells can also be used to both chase away and to attract noncorporeal beings. A loud bell can chase a dangerous spirit away. A sweet bell sound can gather the mind for deeper meditations.

## OTHERS

Other sounds include songs to adjust the *chi*, including karaoke or singing that unifies a group. mantra and prayer can change an environment by removing negative influences and adding positive forces. Singing, whistling a happy tune, and involvement in music can also change your *chi*.

## LIFE

Using life forces involves adding something with vitality, such as living plants or animals, to an area to adjust the *chi*. This can include fish, even the kind of mechanical fish that move electronically, birds or computer screen savers that show moving images of forests, oceans, or animals.

## TREES

Trees add a feeling of living strength; they protect and beautify an area. At the rear of a property they can offer a feeling of support. They connect the area under the ground, on the surface, and reach upward toward the sky, thereby linking Heaven and Earth.

Black Sect Feng Shui classifies the trees into five basic tree shapes connected with the five elements, which are similar to the hill shapes of the five elements.

Large or old trees can be especially sacred, because they can become the dwellings of spirits, ghosts, or tree dragons who feel a sense of security and comfort in lodging there. People can have special connections with trees of life, God trees, or "soul trees." While trees are generally considered good, there are good and bad tree situations.

- Trees can be used as a screen or hedge to protect against many negative influences, like sharp arrows of *chi* pointed to your house. A tree that is luxuriant in growth indicates the good Earth *chi* of that location.

- If a tree blocks your exit, it may be a harmful influence, though less so than square columns or pillars in a similar position. The distance from the

door is important in evaluating the influence. As a good rule of thumb, the tree should not be closer than twice an occupant's height. However, you can also base this distance on the feeling you get: Is it oppressive or open?

- If the trees at the exit of your home make for a narrowing path, trim them back to produce a feeling that your path widens as you approach the world.

- If a tree has been cut and a stump remains, you may plant ivy on the tree, or place a potted plant on the stump to transform the feeling of death and blockage to a feeling of new life and growth.

- A dead, dying, or blocking tree at the entrance is especially bad for older family members or workers. For those over sixty, the influence may be bad for health or indicate a financial crisis.

- If the trees are lush around your house, it is good; if they suddenly die, beware a change for the worse in your luck.

- A large tree behind your house with leaves and branches that hover above your house may give a feeling of protection. Often, however, if trees touch the walls or block windows the effect is that of draining good *chi*. Such trees should be cut back.

Trees that are alive and well located in front of the front door, far enough away from the door so you don't feel the tree is in your way are good, especially, if they give a feeling of guarding. Trees at the front of the house can be planted in symmetrical groups of three, six, or nine units of trees. If you are placing a tree to block a corner, or to blunt the influence of an arrowlike road or a cul-de-sac, visualize that the sharp or draining *chi* coming in is fully moderated by that tree.

Trees around the house are associated with the bones of those who live there. If you need to cut or prune a tree, you should choose, if possible, an auspicious day to remove the tree. Mix a small package of cinnabar (sulfide of mercury) with high-proof liquor and rice. Sprinkle three handfuls of the mixture around the tree to be cut, visualizing that nothing will cut, break bones, or otherwise hurt us or those connected personally with us. Visualize that the tree's life energy will go to a place where its condition will be better and that the life essence of the tree will be happy there. Use the Three Secret Reinforcements detailed above. If you are just trimming limbs you can flick a mixture of cinnabar and liquor onto the limbs with the same visualization. If you are transplanting a tree you can use the same method.

THE TREES
ON TRUMP TOWER

BONSAI

Bonsai are a very concentrated form of life force, containing years of cultivated power. However, it is important that the bonsai were created by cultivation and not by torture, such as by being bound by wire or nutritionally starved. They can represent new hope. Sometimes if people are very sick, bonsai will aid them more than ordinary plants.

## FLOWERS

Flowers represent beauty fully expressed. They are short lived but have an immediate effect in enlivening an environment. (More information on flowers is provided later in this book.)

## FISH TANKS

Fish tanks are used to create a sense of peacefulness and also as an encouragement for wealth. It is good to place a fish tank at eye level so people can easily see the fish and touch the tank.

A special method using goldfish encourages wealth. You may use eight orange and one black goldfish or eight black and one orange goldfish or nine black goldfish. Place them in a tank in the *hsun* position of your living room. Empower this installation with the Three Secret Reinforcements to encourage better money circumstances.

## OTHERS

Plants are similar to trees and are especially useful indoors. A plant can be used to adjust a trigram position if it is missing or to strengthen a particular area of life.

- A green plant in the *chyan* position may help with benefactors.

- A plant in the *kan* position may encourage business.

- You may use three plants to distribute life energy throughout a house. One

plant should be visible as you enter the home, either inside or outside the front door. Another should be seen prominently in the living room. A third should be present in a highly visible location in the master bedroom.

- You may also use nine new plants for this method. Three of them should be placed as described. The others should be put along the path from the entry to the bedroom and also along other main paths of movement. The three or nine plants can adjust the *chi* of Wood. Visualize that the Wood element for that family or enterprise will be adjusted to the right level, achieving greater flexibility, stronger opinions, or more benevolence as is correct for the needs of that situation.

## DYNAMIC PROCESSES

Adding moving objects is a way to adjust *chi*.

### WINDMILLS

Windmills can raise the *chi*, generate momentum, transform an impact, or impart a secret power or meaning as the windmill blades turn. For example, you can place a windmill in the *hsun* position to assist wealth. If the windmill is set but the blades don't turn, money will be kept. If the blades move, the money will come in faster. Fans can be used in a similar fashion.

### WINDSOCKS AND FLAGS

Windsocks, whirlybirds, kites, prayer flags—all use movement to convey a message and to activate *chi*. True Tibetan prayerflags, with tall mastlike wood-

en poles supporting them, can be used to transform a large environment, especially if skillfully placed along ridgelines or in natural wind tunnels. Windsocks and similar moving objects give a feeling of buoyancy and dispense a feeling of energetic flow.

Flags are an excellent way of lifting *chi*. Use flags in a situation where you want to lift the *chi* of a daytime enterprise, the time in which the flags are most visible. The flag of the United States of America is a powerful Feng Shui tool, rarely objected to by tenant associations. Flags may be used to represent the Five Element Processes, the Six True Words, the rainbow spectrum, or to complete an organic color pattern. For more information, see the section on using color .

## FOUNTAINS

Fountains can bring in money, peacefulness, and harmony. Exterior fountains can give a feeling of life, joy, and beauty as you leave home. It is good if the fountain jet angles slightly toward your home or front door. Fountains can also be used to adjust for cul–de–sacs. Fountains can have a cooling effect in a home.

## WATERFALLS

Waterfalls are positive. Preferably the fall is toward the house. A waterfall or a pond flowing from the *hsun* position toward a house is very good. A waterfall's power is increased if the water of the fall is collected in a pool that embraces the house or is moved correctly in a water course and is then recycled.

# OTHERS

## WEATHER VANES

Weather vanes can be used to lift the *chi* of a building. If roads cross or if there is a draining Earth *chi* pattern, weather vanes can be placed on a roof and placed in fixed position so that the area pointed at is "magnetized" by the weather vane, undoing the potential problem.

## FANS

To strengthen and lift the *chi* of a home, place a nonworking fan on the roof, blades facing upward. Interior fans can also be circulators and lifters of *chi*.

## WEIGHT

Adding something heavy, or symbolically heavy, is a good example of how to use the Minor Additions category of weight.

## YU

The *yu* is a small Chinese inkpot. Because stones are often placed within, it symbolizes something heavy, like the weight of the Earth.

If a door is in the bad position of being behind a bed (and the sleepers insist on it remaining there), place a *yu* under the foot of the bed where the feet of the people or person who sleep there lie. The *yu* should contain approximately three-quarters water and nine small stones. Attach the *yu* with a red string from that position to the *kun* position of the bed, which is the upper right ninth of the bed, based upon the *kan* line or foot of the bed. The red string is put underneath the *yu*. Visualize that the people will be safe, that one won't flee, that they will be able to stay together. (Another solution that could be applied, if there is a refusal to move the bed, is to add vines or artificial plants or a three-dimensional collection of the twelve animals of the Chinese zodiac to the door.)

You can also use a *yu* on your desk. Choose the trigram position you wish to stabilize; for example, *kun* for marriage, *hsun* for wealth. If you wish to adjust your *kan* position, the *yu* can rest in the *li* position opposite the *kan* position.

## HEAVY OR MASSIVE ROCKS

These can be used to stabilize a situation, to slow *chi* and thus to bring it in, or to help the *chi* roll back up from a downslope.

## STATUES

A statue represents something heavy and personifies an image. A statue of a Buddha or a deity like Kuan yin (the goddess of Mercy), Jesus, Saint Francis, or the Virgin Mary can have great power, by being a spiritual reminder, a lifter of *chi*, or the stabilizer of the *chi* when placed in a particular trigram.

## FIRECRACKERS

The firecrackers most used in Feng Shui are fake but have the look of real ones. Firecrackers, which symbolize potential explosive force, add protection or power. Placed over a door, in groups of five or nine, they can obviate unexpected bad things. They promote rapid development, fame, and wealth. In a bedroom they provide safety. In an office they represent accomplishment of your wishes and responsibilities. In a room of negative spiritual energy they can provide support and keep a person from harm. Firecrackers can also energize lazy people. If firecrackers seem too Asian for your decor, put them inside a basket of flowers.

In a handgun-shaped house, the position of the "trigger" is very important because it represents the position of the gun and therefore the house. You could position imitation Chinese firecrackers at the trigger position to energize this shape. The play of a famous playwright who employed this technique soon after had a successful Broadway run!

## ARROWHEADS

If you encounter a situation where there is a whirlpool-like draining of *chi*, perhaps caused by a downward-turning staircase near a front door, you can hide arrows or arrowheads under the carpets, pointing the arrows at the staircase to stabilize and adjust the draining effect.

# COLOR

Colors are vital to Feng Shui and are used as general conditioners of all aspects of life. An individual color may be chosen because it expresses your nature, *chi*, or feeling. You may use them freely according to feeling, intuition, and knowledge. Color can influence clothing, food, housing, self-cultivation, transportation, and recreation. Sarah Rossbach and Professor Lin's *Living Color* explores Black Sect color theory in detail.

## FIVE ELEMENT THEORY

You may use the colors of the Five Elements:

|   |   |   |
|---|---|---|
| white (Metal) | green (Wood) | black (Water) |
| red (Fire) | brown or yellow (Earth) | |

You may employ these colors in either the production order or overcoming order, or you can match colors to yourself, your environment, and your companions. A prominent psychologist colored the walls, floor, and ceiling of her office in pastel versions of the Six True Words colors. Her clients appreciated the feeling of peace and blessing.

# THE SIX TRUE WORDS

The Six True Words are the mantra of Avalokitesvara, Chenrezig, Kwan Yin, or Kannon (the Bodhisattva of Compassion). Each syllable is connected with a color:

**Om** White
**Ma** Red
**Ni** Yellow
**Pad** Green
**Me** Blue
**Hum** Black

These six colors express the power of the prayer.

Six flags, one of each color, can be used to represent the power of the mantra. When you move, such flags can come with you in procession from the old house to the new one, bringing with them the positive aspects of the old home and invigorating with blessings the new residence.

## THE EIGHT TRIGRAMS

The Colors of the *ba kua* positions are associated with the Eight Trigrams. You can use color to adjust a trigram position by using the trigram's own color.

| Chen | Green or blue (Wood element) |
| Hsun | Blue or green and red together (or purple) |
| Li | Red (Fire element) |
| Kun | Red and white together (or pink) |
| Tui | White (Metal element) |
| Chyan | Gray or white and black in combination |
| Kan | Black (Water element) |
| Ken | Midnight blue |

For a problem connected with the trigram *tui* in your home, such as completing a project, pneumonia, or a problem with your child, a basic approach is to strengthen that area using white. You could have a Chinese ink painting or calligraphy, so that the white of the paper produces the black of the ink, to adjust *tui*, with the refinement of using the productive element order sequence, Metal produces Water.

You can use the colors of the trigrams in combination with the elements. For example, you could use white in the *kan* position, which is connected with Water, because white (Metal) produces black (Water).

## RAINBOW COLORS

The rainbow spectrum, a powerful natural force, represents the energy centers of the human body in Indian and Buddhist culture. In Black Sect meditations, we use the rainbow spectrum in visualization and meditation. Seeing a rainbow means good fortune. Symbolic in the West of the covenant and in Buddhism of perfection, the rainbow spectrum can be employed in Feng Shui design to enhance an environment.

# THE ORGANIC MODEL

The colors of a tree used in sequence—brown for the trunk, green for the leaves, red and yellow for the flowers and fruit—can cure Feng Shui problems. For example, if your bedroom is above a garage, the yin condition of sleep may be detrimentally connected with the yin environment below. You could paint the garage brown, lay a green carpet on the bedroom floor, and use flowered pink wallpaper on the bedroom walls, following the organic patterns of a tree to avoid the confusion, disturbance, and other difficulties of having a bedroom above a garage.

## FRAGRANCE

Smell is related in the brain to memory. What we smell upon entering will affect how we perceive a site. If the first smell we receive is of a disinfectant or the too pervasive smell of food or the smell of fear, we will be affected negatively. If the smell is bad, use flowers or the fragrances discussed below to change the luck.

## INCENSE

Incense is an important source of fragrance. Offering incense can be practiced as meditation and as divination.

## ORANGE PEELS

1.  Carry in your pocket or purse nine pieces of orange peel cut into circles. Empower the nine peels to provide you with yang and auspicious chi. As needed, refresh yourself by taking the pieces out and

smelling them. Take the orange peels with you when you go to the hospital, visit a sick friend, attend a funeral, are exposed to strong yin *chi,* or when practicing Feng Shui.

2.   Break nine pieces of orange peel into smaller pieces. Sprinkle them in every room around the house in every room holding your hand palm up as you toss peels. Walk around the house in a clockwise direction. Visualize that auspicious *chi* is filling the whole house, eliminating or liberating all inauspicious *chi.* Positive *chi* fills the house like sunlight or spiritual light. For a large house you may use nine oranges taking nine round slices from each orange. You may end by chanting the Six True Words (*Om Ma Ni Pad Me Hum*) visualizing all bad *chi* has been driven away or transformed into pure *chi* as part of your completion of this purification with the Three Secret Reinforcements. (See Removing Bad *Chi*  to learn how to use this powerful purification method involving burning dried aged tangerine peel.)

## FRAGRANT FLOWER METHOD

The flower method is a wonderful way to remove obstacles that impede forward progress in life, to unstick areas of life that are stuck, and to create a sense of joy. Empower this method, as well, to invite local spirits and nature spirits to enter your environment with positive energy and improve your luck.

Beginning on an auspicious day, or within three days of reading about this method, every third day, for twenty-seven consecutive days, bring a new bouquet of fragrant flowers into your home or business. Place the flowers in the major rooms. Keep each bouquet in place for at least three days or longer. (Discard the flowers when they begin to deteriorate.)

At home, you may use the master bedroom, living room, and kitchen as the primary rooms for placing bouquets. You may also include other bedrooms or the study. In an office, place the flowers where people relax, perhaps a kitchen area or conference room or other rooms that will be used most frequently.

Carry this method out using different flowers (some of which must be fragrant) so that no two bouquets in the sequence are identical. It is best to use different kinds of fragrant flowers. When you put a bouquet in place, use the Three Secret Reinforcements, visualizing clearly the desired results. With each bouquet visualize that the *chi* of the room is being perfectly adjusted. You may practice this method for nine sets of three days (twenty-seven days) or include an additional placement on the twenty-seventh day for a total of ten bouquets. If you must leave during the time period, you may begin the practice again from the first step when you return.

## TOUCH

Rearranging furniture and decorating a home involve changing the experience of touch. Fabrics, carpets, personal dress all offer the ability to adjust touch. One ancient Chinese way to adjust *chi* through the sense of touch was the "magic bag." A lethargic or otherwise distracted individual would be asked to reach into a bag. Within it would be a simulated snake. The experience of shock could adjust that person's *chi*. You may also place something that feels like a snake, fuzzy worms, or a chicken head on a place you habitually touch, like a banister or doorknob. As you grasp the unfamiliar object, your self-protective instincts and your ability to fight for yourself is aroused.

You may also use the process of touch to activate a residence. After unifying with divine *chi*, select twenty-seven objects that have been unmoved for a year, like beds, dining tables, and clocks. Slightly move or raise these objects. At that exact moment visualize that the areas pressed under these items begin to move. Reinforce with the Three Secrets, visualizing the entire space is revitalized with auspicious *chi*. All sense of pressure departs; all bad *chi* leaves.

## OTHER OBJECTS

### BEADED CURTAIN

A beaded curtain can serve as a door in an area that has a negative empty door.

### CHINESE BAMBOO FLUTE

The proper flute for Feng Shui is the *hsiao*. It is an end-blown bamboo flute cut from the root with the joints visible.

- Flutes provide a message of peace and safety. (Bamboo has a very peaceful feeling.)

- The flute offers support with its force. It can be relied upon to help you. It gives support in difficulties.

- The sword shape of flutes fight off evil. The red ribbon such flutes come with represent a sword hanger.

- The joints of the flute increase in size as you go up from the root. The flute, therefore, represents step-by-step improvement.

- The flute can be hung in a trigram position. A flute hung in the *hsun* position aids wealth, while one hung in the *kun* position helps marriage. Flutes are hung mouthpiece up, at a 45-degree angle to the ceiling. Two flutes suggest the octagon shape that represents the Eight Trigrams, the *ba kua*. A flute can also connect two trigrams. A flute hung in the *hsun* position, if parallel to a rectangular wall, also draws upon the *ken* position. A flute in the *kun* position also draws upon or is in relation with the *chyan* position.

- A flute is used as a pointer, to focus *chi*.

- A flute drives away negative persons.

- Other aspects: If you feel pressured from above, perhaps in a basement apartment, you can take four flutes and hang them straight up, with the mouthpiece toward the ceiling, in each corner to resolve this problem. A flute beneath your spine, with the mouthpiece at your head, can greatly help with back problems. (The flute is placed between the box spring and the mattress or just under the mattress.) A flute used to represent peace and safety doesn't have to be big. But if you were to use a flute to offset overhanging beams, then the size of the flute should be large. Hang two flutes vertically or in *ba kua* relationship below each end of the beam.

## TEN COINS OF CHING DYNASTY

The *Shi Di*, the Ten Emperors' Otherworldly Cure, involves hanging up a physical representation of the the ten coins of the reigns of each of the Ching or

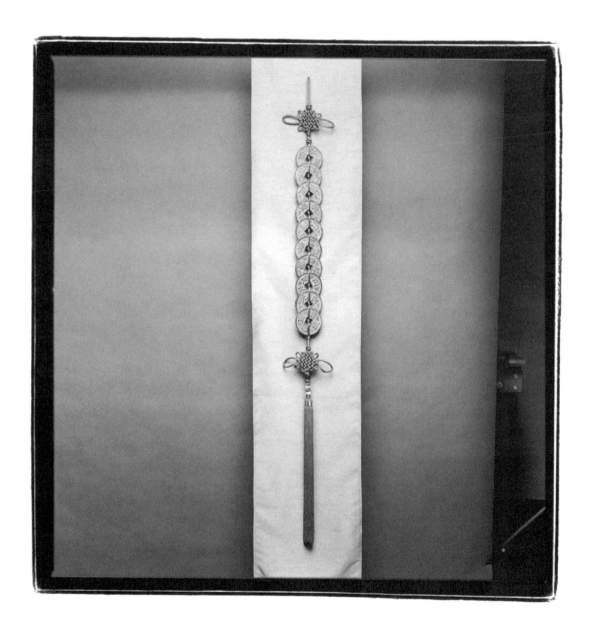

Manchu emperors. The coins symbolize the treasury and national reserve of each of the Ching emperors. The ten coins, affixed to an imperial yellow cloth, block evil, make for wealth, and bring safety. You may put the *Shi Di* in the *hsun* position to influence wealth. Use the *hsun* positions of your office, master bedroom, or living room. You can also use this method to adjust a missing *hsun* position. You can place the *Shi Di* in the *kun* Position, to find a wealthy person to marry. In this way you link a wealth attractor with a position connected with marriage. In the *kan* position, the *Shi Di* will encourage money from a successful career. If you put the Ten Emperor Coins in *tui* position, your children may get your money. Placed in the *chen* position, money may come to you from family members.

The *Shi Di* is best kept in an eye-catching spot, a place that is visible upon entering a home or workplace. The ten coins of the Ching dynasty cure can also help people become more upright. Their money will come from more honorable and less questionable sources.

When using the Method of Minor Additions, remember that good Feng Shui should be practiced with appreciation for individual sense of style and beauty. The effectiveness of the minor additions will be furthered by attention to timing, qualities, novelty, or unique appropriateness of the method used, size, scale, and personal meaning.

Good Feng Shui cures are like good cooking. Use the Method of Minor Additions with precision, enjoying, as you apply these recipes, both the cooking and the eating.

THE ROLE OF THE EXPERT
THOUGHTS FOR THE BEGINNER
HOME
FENG SHUI FROM THE PERSPECTIVE OF BLACK SECT TANTRIC
BUDDHISM: A STRUCTURAL OVERVIEW
THE ARRANGEMENT OF OBJECTS AND THE NATURE OF THE HOME
FENG SHUI AND THE WORKPLACE

# FENG SHUI AT HOME AND WORK

## THE ROLE OF THE EXPERT

Feng Shui experts hear things that people may only tell their physicians, lawyers, counselors, psychologists, priests, bartenders, or hairdressers. They handle and possess secret knowledge. A true expert has the ability to read and adjust your *chi*. When you have a problem that you cannot fix on your own, the expert's ability to see your life in a more objective way without imposing preconceptions may be just what you need.

The good judgment of the Feng Shui practitioner and the importance of addressing Feng Shui problems in the appropriate sequence is critical. In the Talmud it is said that if you wish a man could acquire land and a house and a wife and children, it is a blessing. But if you wish those things in the reverse order it is a curse. Therefore it is imperative that you have a knowledgeable practitioner.

## RED ENVELOPES

Custom dictates that the provider of a transcendental Feng Shui solution should receive a red envelope. The red envelope must contain money.

Red, the color of life blood, represents vitality and auspiciousness and, like fire, can burn up all bad things. The envelope serves like an ancient shield to protect the transmitter of secret knowledge from absorbing the problem solved or otherwise coming to harm. For example, if you come to me with a personal problem to receive a transcendental method, the red envelope protocol may avert my taking on your problem, especially at the level of *chi*. The red envelopes protect oneself when helping others.

Giving 1, 3, 9, 27, 81, 99, or 108 red envelopes is particularly correct. Generally, at least one red envelope is given for each secret method provided. The money put in the envelope is not only symbolic but also represents the giver of the envelope and shows respect for the tradition and appreciation for the value of the method being shared.

## FENG SHUI GUIDELINES

Ultimately, there are no rules for a Feng Shui consultation. There are, however, guidelines I follow and teach, which make Feng Shui effective and user friendly. Combining Western and Asian methods make a good framework for seeking the understanding needed to serve a client well.

If I were to visit you to do a Feng Shui consultation for your home or workplace, I would want to know who you are. We would discuss in detail what life issues are most important to you. After completing the site survey I would assess your Feng Shui needs in relation to personal *chi* and the dynamics of the home or workplace. Combined with astrology, observation, and intuition, understanding the Eight Trigrams in a life helps discern personal *chi*. I ask a client to consider in detail the areas of life covered by the Eight Trigrams and the *tai chi* Position and to be able to convey in essence what the actual situation is, what may be weak or strong, and what the client would like to achieve in relation to these life areas. By understanding these life issues we can adjust the Feng Shui to help achieve a person's wishes and correct or address any problems our discussion has brought up.

# THOUGHTS FOR THE BEGINNER

To try Black Sect Feng Shui on your own, begin with yourself and your immediate surroundings and circumstances. What affects us most is based upon what is nearest to us. Your own personal *chi* is of primary importance, next being your physical body. Next in importance is your bed. Then your bedroom, home (and secondarily, workplace), street, neighborhood, community, city, state, nation, continent, and world. This principle is effective guidance in transforming your life for the better.

If you want to help others, be sure that you respond only to a direct request for information. If no one asks, don't tell. Revealing the methods described herein involves being like a bell. A soft ring is responded to with a soft sound, a strong ring with a strong sound; therefore, small questions receive small answers, and serious questions receive serious answers.

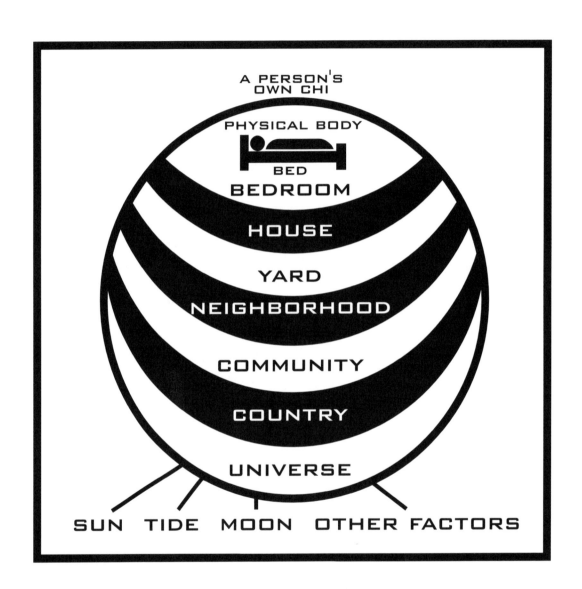

## UNIVERSAL IDEAS IN GEOMANCY

Feng Shui shares many principles, practices, and methods with all schools of geomancy. Among these ideas and methods are:

- Recognizing the importance of the central place, or center of a site, such as the *omphalos* (Greek), *umbilicus* (Latin), *emsa* (Hebrew), or *tai chi* position (Chinese).

- Using the center line of the land shape to direct the flow of *chi*, for the siting of major buildings or as a basic organizing principle. In residences, this line divides the left and the right sides of a house.

- Choosing sites with rising *chi* or creating rising *chi*, which includes the feeling of your body lifted up by brightness, spaciousness, or loftiness, being at the top.

- Choosing places of strong Earth *chi*, which encompass the conditions of fertility, safety, and flow.

- Choosing the commanding position, which is the controlling or dominant position in an area.

- Using the site to make time work for you.

- Using repetition and variation, for example, by doubling what appears in the terrain with an architectural feature, or by balancing, attaching, or adding an outstanding feature or by utilizing rhythm and proportion with symmetry, balance, wholeness, gradation, as between inner and outer, front and back, or from small to big.

- Integrating mundane and transcendent, outer and inner, form and mind (or will); called in Chinese, *sying* and *yi*.

*The Ten Books of Architecture*, written by the Roman architect Vitruvius, can be used as a geomancy textbook. His fundamental principles of architecture, the "six harmonies" below, parallel the universal ideas listed above.

1. **Order** involves adjustment according to quantity, getting the large and the small to correspond.

2. **Arrangement** has to do with relationships between aspects of the site, coordinating, for example, ground plan, elevation, and perspective, so that everything is in its proper place.

3. **Eurythmy** involves coordinating the parts of a house so that height, width, and length are appropriate and create beauty.

4. **Symmetry** comes from using an appropriate standard of scale so that all the small parts are in harmony and they repeat in the way the building is divided, giving us a feeling that this building is like a body made up of congenial parts.

5. **Propriety** comes from choosing a style that suits the nature and use of the building and the site. Propriety includes, for example, knowing how to use natural light.

6. **Economy** employs proper management of materials in keeping with thrift, balancing cost, common sense, and the requirements of the kind of home you're building, whether a country estate or a city apartment.

These six harmonies are guidelines for establishing synergy with universal unity as described by Pythagoras: "There is harmony in the humming of the strings; there is music in the spacing of the spheres."

For Professor Lin, architecture embodies the spatial arts, which include and integrate visual arts and musical qualities in material form. Good architecture is like fine music or wonderful song—it captures rhythm, melody, gradation, and resonance. Chinese architecture and Feng Shui developed parallel to Chinese aesthetic principles. Emphasized are:

- A perfect sense of **completeness** created by the movement of *chi* throughout a design, whether an individual structure or multiple buildings. A sense of smooth flow and eye-pleasing qualities create wholeness and give a complete aesthetic experience.

- Symmetry and balance with the **center line** of a site.

- **Order,** or a sense of correctness obtained through adjustment of front and back, left and right, either in strict order or by dynamic nonsymmetry.

- **Proportion and rhythm,** or a skillful handling of factors such as foundation, platform, height, and width; the length and thickness of pillars and columns, roof overhang, length, and slope; ceiling in relation to ground plan. These factors give the exteriors of buildings a curving rhythmic line.

- **Yin and yang distinguished.** Outer or more frontal buildings are considered yang. Therefore, these individual structures will use odd numbers (considered yang), for example, five doors for each of three palaces. More inner or interior buildings are regarded as yin. Therefore, their numbers are even, as will be the number of rooms and doors. Beijing's Forbidden Purple City (above) illustrates the yin-yang balance perfectly.

- The "**safe and happy chair.**" Correct, comfortable siting of a building provides protection at the back, support on the sides, and a view to the front. If at your back is a mountain and to the front there is a view of the ocean or a wide and pleasing prospect, the feeling is protected, comfortable, yet expansive.

These universal ideas are echoed in the doctrines of the modern movement in interior design in Edith Wharton and Ogden Codman's *The Decoration of Houses*, which discusses the idea of suitability in the arrangement of rooms and advocates design to encourage the "sweetness of life."

## THE NATURE OF THE HOME

How we live in and think about our home reflects our understanding of comfort. Being at home and feeling at home is important and should give one a similar feeling to the home-team advantage of sports.

Our home environment is a perfect expression of our psychological and spiritual state. It is a wonderful tool to understanding ourselves, and a powerful way to catalyze greater harmony within us to make changes to the home. The material environment does not lie. If we block our movement path or prevent our doors from fully opening or block physical progress through the house, we are providing the universe with a message that we are not ready for complete access to life's bounty. Normal maintenance, cleanliness, beauty, and space have both mundane and transcendental meanings.

# HOME AS BODY, BODY AS SITE

An early Feng Shui text stated that the "body of the Earth is like the body of a human being." Practical applications of this principle include looking at houses, rooms, and sites as if they were people, as well as studying the human body in the same way as you would a site.

## HOW TO UNDERSTAND
## THE HOME AS A BODY

The entire house corresponds to a superimposed image of a human body. The way we apply this image is to imagine that a body lies face down within the house. Its head is positioned at the front door. If, from this perspective, the area connected with the body's right side is shortened or has portions missing, females in the home may suffer. If the corresponding left side has a problem, males may have difficulties.

The electrical system of the house corresponds to blood circulation. The water system relates to the human body's plumbing. The walls are like skin. The front left and right are like your hands. The roof ridge pole is symbolic of both the back and the top of the head. The front door represents the head, but in some cases it also represents the birth canal. If the entry is very narrow, there may be problems in giving birth.

## THE EIGHT TRIGRAMS AND THE BODY

Using the superimposed image of the body as the house, remember that each trigram is associated with a body part: *chyan* is the head, *kan* is the ears, *ken* is the hands, *chen* represents the feet, *hsun* is associated with the hips, *li* is connected with the eyes, *kun* is related to the abdomen and stomach, *tui* is connected with the lungs and mouth. A problem in a part of the house based on the superimposed human image may express itself in terms of the overlay of the trigrams or it may express itself in terms of problems having to do with the portion of the image of the body that is impacted by the shape or other conditions of the house.

## THE THREE MOST IMPORTANT THINGS IN YOUR HOME

The front door, the bed, and the stove or range top are the three most important objects in the home from both traditional and Black Sect perspectives.

- The **front door** represents the way life comes to us, our opportunities, and possibilities. It represents the yang dimension of experience.

- The **bed** where we sleep is energetically connected to each of us. Sleep is a yin condition. That the bed shelters, comforts, and enables us to truly rest illustrates its great importance.

- The **stove** represents the source of our food. For most of us, the ability to obtain food comes from our work in the world. The stove has a great deal to do with our public life, our career, the recognition and notice we receive, and our ability to manifest our wishes.

# FENG SHUI FROM THE PERSPECTIVE OF BLACK SECT TANTRIC BUDDHISM: A STRUCTURAL OVERVIEW

The structure of Black Sect Feng Shui has two sides. One side represents the yang objective, tangible, physical, visible, side of Black Sect Feng Shui. The other side touches on basic methods that involve the yin subjective, intangible, invisible aspect. By combining the objective and subjective aspects, we are able to understand what to evaluate in a Feng Shui site and what methodology to employ to create a successful Feng Shui transformation.

## OBJECTIVE TANGIBLE PHYSICAL VISIBLE

### JUDGING THE QUALITIES OF THE CHI OF THE EARTH

We first look at the way the house in located in its surroundings. Traditional Feng Shui offers a rich vocabulary for understanding the *chi* of the Earth. We look to the mountains and the water of a land to understand its *chi* and fortune. The mountains, with their peaks, ridges, and other forms, are thought of as dragons, which can bring auspicious *chi*. We note distinguishing features that include watercourses, geologic formations, and unusual shapes. We look to the site in question, observing its buildings or graves. We look for what is called the dragon's lair, or the site itself, the focal point of the *chi* of that place, sometimes a small declivity, a hollow, a cave, or an armchair-like place protected on three sides. A traditional ideal site would be the "safe and happy armchair" type site, which is partway up a hill, with the feeling of protection at the back produced by a treed slope, supporting ridges like the arm of a chair, and a wide frontal view.

In general, we want to know how the *chi* enters or leaves a site. We want to know if the *chi* is collected or condensed, perhaps collected on a branch of a river. Alternatively, the *chi* may be dispersed, leaking or running away, perhaps down a slope or off a precipitous drop-off. Perhaps the *chi* may injure or impose on the site by being too direct in its approach or too strong and draining. At a given location everything may be interlocked, mutually contained, or recognized as having a unified pattern. One place may be beautiful, luxuriant, or pure in its *chi*. Another may feel chaotic, confused, or muddy. We want to feel the underlying presence of the place with a sense of sympathy for its feeling, tone, and quality. We can come to know the character of a site and find the rule or pattern which governs its behavior and predicts what may happen. Examples of how to determine the character of the *chi* of your site follow.

## EARTH CHI REFLECTED IN SURROUNDING LIFE

To know the condition of the Earth *chi* of a place is fundamental to understanding its Feng Shui. There are some simple ways of knowing the *chi* of the Earth.

- **Animals.** Consider the animals you see. Are they healthy or weak? What kind of animals are there? Are they auspicious or inauspicious? Making that determination is very culturally based, so be careful. A Chinese example sets a pleasing magpie against a crow. But the crow and raven are oracular birds for the Tibetans and the bird of Saturn in Europe. Deer are considered auspicious. Black cats, especially black cats with four white feet, are definitely considered not auspicious—unless they belong to you. Upon seeing a cat, check its coat, overall health, and its *chi*. Healthy animals indicate a benefiting environment; unhealthy ones may be a warning.

- **Plants.** What is the state of the vegetation? Are the trees lush? What is the growth of trees like, especially for that particular species? Are there areas of discolored vegetation or ragged growth? I once found a cancer in a tree trunk directly in line with where a man suffering from throat cancer lay. A line of discoloration in poorly grown grass led to his window. Underground water problems contributed to the discoloration. Is the growth of the plants on the site better, worse, or the same as on neighboring properties? Evaluating plants and how they grow inside the house is also a way of studying the Earth *chi*.

- **People.** What kind of people are present? Are there many professionals in the neighborhood or are there homeless people? How is the neighborhood changing? Poverty and social activity all have their own *chi*. You can also use the *chi* of a location. There is a Chinese saying that if you stay by the color black, you yourself will become black. For example, those who haven't yet been able to have children could choose to live in a place that has many children, where life is teeming, thereby increasing their chances.

- **Events.** You may consider what events have transpired in the neighboring houses or apartments. Have there been car accidents? Robberies? Deaths? Arguments? Bankruptcy? Or have there been births? Promotions? Increases in salary? Successful undertakings?

- **Spiritual events.** When you visit a site to evaluate its Feng Shui, what happens while you are there is extremely important. In Professor Lin's example, if, when you arrive at a site, you find that parking is prevented by a gathering funeral and two hearses have parked in front of the "auspicious house for sale" you are visiting; that when you try to enter, the door sticks and the key breaks; that when you turn on the light, the bulb blows; that there are dead birds on the deck and scurrying cockroaches in the kitchen, it may well be that this is not the house for you. You might even fall and get hurt on the stairs when you try to run away.

We need to understand how the *chi* gets connected, how one event expresses and relates to others. This allows us to interpret spiritual events as indicators of the *chi* of a place. If you just see one thing, in terms of the Earth *chi*, it is not enough. In looking at the *chi* of the land, be flexible and innovative. It is also good to mentally step back and take a wide view of that place thinking about the city, ecosystem, water and mountains—all the wider factors that influence the *chi* of an area.

## EARTH CHI INFLUENCED BY NATURAL TERRAIN

External influences are also part of an Earth *chi* analysis. One such consideration is the path from one's house to one's work. If the way is dry, dirty, or through graveyards, junkyards, slums, or past funeral homes, you may get to work and dwell on dead friends or your own imminent death. For some people this influence may even be more profound. Throughout the day you may be depressed. This kind of experience may present career obstacles and prevent a person from breaking through to success. If, on the other hand, you see trees and lush vegetation on the way to work, or pass by schools or activities promising prosperity, you have a different, more positive, influence.

The plot of land we occupy is the immediate environment and outer boundary between us and the world. Both traditional Feng Shui schools and Professor Lin analyze plot shapes in great detail. In this book we will approach plot shape from several standpoints including:

- *chi* of the area;

- the Eight Trigrams;

- the way the shape accommodates a real or imagined, natural or man-made object, such as a chair;

- how the house or lot approximates a human body.

You must learn to judge the plot shape, the shape of the house, and its rooms by learning how to superimpose the Eight Trigrams discussed here. In this way you will know if areas in an irregular plot are projections, and thus strengtheners, or if such areas represent missing sections, which need to be corrected so that the areas of life that correspond to them are not negatively impacted.

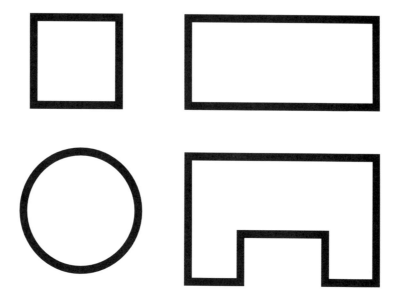

In general rectangles, squares, and circles are considered very good shapes because they are complete and bring positive *chi* to the home. It is excellent if the plot is deep—that is to say, long rather than wide—because it can receive and hold more *chi* than a plot that is wide but not deep. A narrow front with a wide rear, which is a shape like a money bag, is good. A wide front and a narrow rear is a dustbin shape, which allows money to flow out and may cause bad events to enter your life. If you are reading this and live in a dustbin-shaped plot, don't be discouraged. Apply the Method of Minor Additions techniques described earlier, including flags or lights in the back corners of the plot or a mirror on the interior back wall to fix this problem.

Three-dimensional plot shapes can influence the *chi* of a plot. For example, a piece of land in the shape of the Chinese brush holder, which is traditionally associated with scholarly and literary work, will help develop knowledgeable people who will be successful. Land like a lion's head may promote courage, heroism, military prowess, or help create a religious leader. It is good to be on top of, but not in, the lion's mouth. A mountain shaped like a profile of the Goddess of Mercy, Kuan Yin, will encourage compassion. (A perfect example of this shape is Mount Tamalpais.)

Man-made shapes can add positive influences. A scorpion shape is considered auspicious because it is powerful. You might enhance such a shape if you activate the claws and stinger with flags or lights or perhaps add red brick and flowers to create claws and lighted bricks to create the tail. Two dragons playing with a pearl is a land formation of great promise because that space gathers the power of the dragon. Utilizing the piece of land that is the pearl can yield great power. If two hills suggest a dragon, you could create a pearl by adding a pool or fountain.

Although the explanation is too complex for an introductory guidebook, some plot and house shapes are designed around the Eight Trigrams and their relationship with the animals of the Chinese zodiac. For example, a special plot shape suggests a lightning bolt. In this case build near the top of the bolt to foster rapid and continued progress.

Both Earth *chi* and plot shape may need adjustment. While some solutions to situations are described herein, every situation is unique. Your solution should creatively employ the principles described. For example, if the Earth *chi* is not good in a rectangular plot, you may place four plants or trees in the corners, or add spotlights in the corners aimed toward the center.

A house on a slope with its main door below the road is subject to pressures

that tend to adversely affect career and money. It is better to live above the road and avoid that pressure, so that career, money, and children can more easily flourish.

If the plot shape is irregular, then it is necessary to use it to your advantage, perhaps applying the method of approximating the shape to a real or imagined, natural or man-made object.

## THE MOUNTAIN

*The Five Peaks are but one chi blown by a vast breathing.*—Chu Hsi

Around the year 880 C.E. in Jiangshi Province, the founder of the School of Forms wrote about "The Twelve Stave Patterns" as a basic description of the *chi* of mountains, dividing them into twelve basic types, each of which had seventeen variations. The first three basic types are valuable here:

- **Shun** means concurrent, or with it. In terms of flow, the term means auspicious in acupuncture. The site receives the influence of the *chi* by riding along with the mountain's incoming vein. An example is Boulder, Colorado.

- **Ni** means anticurrent. The site receives the influence "inversely" by meeting the root mountain's vein head on.

- **Shu** means coiled up. Here, the site is on an inner range, surrounded by higher peaks, and receives the chi in a coiled up manner so that it can gather at the site.

At a given site the *chi* may be rising, lifting our spirits, but may not be suit-

able for human use. For example, mighty Mount Shasta in California represents the wild, undifferentiated power of primordial place and primordial mind and would not be a suitable environment for your home. Mount Tamalpais, near San Francisco, is the prototype of the humanizing mountain, in which the intensity of the root is harmonized and expressed in ways that shelter and nurture human life.

## THE DRAGON AS AN IMAGE OF CHI

For Feng Shui, the dragon is an image of the flow of *chi* in nature and is commonly used to describe ridges and mountains. *The Burial Book*, which coined the term Feng Shui, describes its movement and its presence at a perfect site:

> *The Dragon's march and stopping place are easy to espy.*
> *When it marches, all the hills seem to fly;*
> *When it stops, it's just as if a man should lie or sit*
> *Encircling hills, embracing waters: here's the perfect fit.*
> *—translated by Andrew March*

In China, mountains and rivers were deeply involved in both official Imperial religion and popular religion. The mountain was appreciated in terms of its sacred power. In places as separate as Japan and ancient Crete, the influence of the mountain was trusted to sustain the culture of the city by coordinating its power with seasonal activity and the city's design.

In the *I Ching*, (Book of Changes), the trigram connected with mountain *ken* denotes self–knowledge and cultivation, skillfulness in handling situations, meditation, and in the human body, the hand. The *ken* trigram combines the male principle at the top (the unbroken line) "which strives upward by its nature" with "the female principle [which] is below since the direction of its movement is downward. Thus there is rest . . . ."

"The keeping still of the mountain balances rest and movement . . . in agreement with the demands of the time." The phrase "keeping still" means knowing when to stop. But this stopping includes the potential for a new beginning. For "movement and stillness depend on each other. . . . Because one stillness pervades inside and outside, it is called mountain."

## HILLS

The most basic designation of hill shapes are the round, square, and triangle formations. Hill shapes may also be understood in terms of the expression of the Five Element Processes.

When we discuss three–dimensional plot shapes, we will further discuss how hill shapes may be approximated to real or imagined, natural or man-made objects. For example, the ideal armchair-type site emphasizes a protective hill or slope to the rear. It is called the "black tortoise." To the right are supporting hills or ridges called the "white tiger." To the left supporting hills or ridges are called the "green dragon." There should be a view to the front with a small hill called the "red bird."

# BLACK SECT FENG SHUI HILL SHAPES

1. This situation represents a hill that is too steep for successful siting of a home.

3. This situation is similar to the previous one but less extreme.

2a. In this case the position of the door is critical.

4. In this case, placing the door on the flat side of the slope is much more desirable.

2b. If the door faces the downslide view, it is good. If the door faces the blocking upsweep side, it is a difficult Feng Shui positioning.

5a. The building on top of the hill is not good; the hill is too steep and exposed.

6a. The house sited on a slope below the road is poorly placed. If the door faces the road it is even worse.

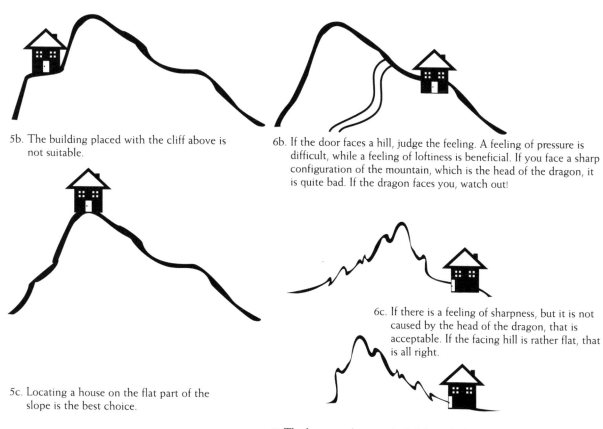

5b. The building placed with the cliff above is not suitable.

6b. If the door faces a hill, judge the feeling. A feeling of pressure is difficult, while a feeling of loftiness is beneficial. If you face a sharp configuration of the mountain, which is the head of the dragon, it is quite bad. If the dragon faces you, watch out!

6c. If there is a feeling of sharpness, but it is not caused by the head of the dragon, that is acceptable. If the facing hill is rather flat, that is all right.

5c. Locating a house on the flat part of the slope is the best choice.

7. The house at the top of a hill has a feeling of instability. The house at the bottom of a steep hill, which overhangs above it, is subject to a "tiger's jaw" or "dragon's claw." This is a very bad Feng Shui positioning.

# BLACK SECT FENG SHUI SLOPE SITUATIONS

1. This house is placed on a slope that is too steep. Add a wood deck to provide a sense of scope and to relieve the precipitous feeling.

2a. This placement, midway on the slope, is OK.

2b. Placement nearer the top of the slope is fine.

3. This house is positioned appropriately.

4. In this situation add trees to make the *chi* of the gentle slope rise and roll back. The distance between the house and the trees behind it should be sufficiently wide.

5. This slope position is mediocre.

6. Near the tail end of the slope, this position is weak.

7. Here there is a dangerous fall-off. Protective measures are required.

8. Although near the tail end of the slope, the lush vegetation with its strong Earth *chi* at the surface helps greatly.

Water, called "the blood of the universe," is the most responsive of natural elements. When the wind blows, the ripples that appear on the water disclose the "natural organic pattern," the beautiful form that evidences water's adaptability and its expressiveness of *chi*.

Water is associated with wisdom, money, and the social context. The reference to money applies to the slang usage of the term Feng Shui (or "wind" and "water") as a synonym for gambling, meaning to blow your money away.

## RIVERS, STREAMS, AND WATERCOURSES

Generally, if water flows toward your site or curves toward you embracing the site, it is considered good. If a house faces water this, generally, is good. A main watercourse that divides into two or more watercourses is often negative because it indicates dispersion of force. Sharp bends forming "straight arrows" are considered not good. In general, if water flows without break from the front to the back of a site it is desirable.

The *Water Dragon Classic*, dating to about 600 C.E. states: "If water pours away from a site, it drains off and is hurried, how can it be abundant and water accumulate? If it comes in straight and goes out straight it injures men. Darting left the eldest son meets with misfortune, darting right the youngest son meets with calamity."

Watercourses are classified as trunks and branches. The *hsueh* (your home, the site, the dragon's lair or cave) should nestle among branch watercourses, subsidiary flows rather than the main trunk. Water is the path of *chi*, and inner branches stop and gather *chi*. The more branches of a river, the more *chi* to be gathered. The big rivers are the arteries or pulses of the Earth. Don't, however, site too close to the main branch; water runs by too fast to allow the gentle penetration of *chi* at the site.

Slow meanders are usually better than rapid flow because they allow the *chi* to penetrate the property, unless the scale of the property is large enough to accommodate rapidly flowing *chi* comfortably. A house should be above the water and far enough away to avoid damage to the foundation.

The trigram position of water is important. Water in *kan*, *chen*, or *hsun* usually benefits. Water in *li* may be difficult. Water in *ken*, *kun*, or the *tai chi* position is problematic. Water in *chyan* or *tui* can be used helpfully.

This example shows a classic situation of inner or interior *chi*. The inner water branches also embrace the site.

# LAKES, PONDS, AND POOLS

The house should be more significant than a lake, pond, or pool. If a house is sited near a large lake, its distance should be sufficiently far from the water. The placement of a pool or pond should be well considered. A square or rectangular shape for a pond is fine if flat edges face the house. Desirable shapes include a circle, a half circle with the straight edge facing the house, an omega, a crescent, or a kidney.

If the pointed edge of a pond faces a front, rear, or side door, this is not good. If it is angled toward the walls of the house, it is not as bad. Place a potted plant between the point of the pond and the house. If the point faces the front door one's head might be adversely affected. Empower with the three Secret Reinforcements to remove any negative effect.

You could also employ a pool shape that corresponds with the part of the body associated with the trigram and that coordinates with the sequences and water shapes of the Five Elements. A water feature in the *hsun* position can be helpful in terms of money. A pond in the *hsun* position can utilize a kidney shape with the curve embracing the house. (*Hsun* is connected with the kidney area in the body.) A crescent-shape pond embracing the house, oriented to the front door, is especially good for wealth, good health, offering great potential for prosperous development.

A pond, hot tub, or swimming pool is much better in the *hsun* position than in the *li* position. (*Li* is associated with Fire.) That Water puts out Fire makes this positioning inauspicious. If this is your situation you can resolve the problem by the skillful use of color. You could paint a wall yellow or brown so that, in Five Element language, Earth separates the Water and Fire (symbolically, Earth destroys the Water thus protecting the Fire position). You may also use the color green so Water enhances Wood, which then enhances the *li* or Fire position. You can paint the inside of the pool or add nine green plants or trees. Remember to use the Three Secret Reinforcements.

## WASTE WATER

If waste water flows away from the front of the house it is not as good as if it flows out to the back. If it does flow out to the front, if possible, make it turn back to the house at least for a little space before it flows away. If you can't control the flow of waste water, throw rice mixed with liquor and cinnabar on the egress point visualizing that any problems to health, wealth, relationships, study, benefactors, and opportunities are resolved. Use the Three Secrets. You may also put a plant with some rice placed inside it on the manhole cover of the waste water run-off.

## EARTH CHI INFLUENCED BY MAN-MADE TERRAIN

### ROADS AND STREETS

Roads have much the same influence as the flow of water. Many of the same basic rules apply. The Feng Shui of slopes also applies to streets and roads. Feng Shui learning involves knowing how to recognize these similarities. As was said for water embracing, qualities such as flowing toward one, facing a stream or street, confluence, and elevation are good, while curving away, running away, diverging, or sharp angles of flow are difficult.

If a road embraces a house (1.), curving toward it, hugging it, the situation favors good finances, success for children, and plans realized. If the road curves away from the house (2.), it is easy to lose money or to see opportunities but not be able to grasp them.  Make use of the Minor Additions Method and place a mirror outside on top of the door jamb or inside the house on a wall you will see as you enter to symbolically bring the out-curving road into the house. If the road that curves away is your own driveway the negative effect is less. Still, add a mirror.

A classic negative situation is the T-intersection (3.), where the long arm of the T aims at your house. It is a common folk belief in Chinese culture that this situation is negative. The intensity of the flow of *chi* toward one's own home will harm health, finances, and relationships. You can make use of a *ba-kua* (Eight Trigrams) mirror to reflect the linear force away. But other solutions are possible. A beautiful and very powerful one is the Mount Tai talisman.

I had advised a family that it was all right to move into a T-intersection home. The arm of the T sloped away from the house, as did the *chi*, strongly mitigating the theoretically dangerous *chi* flow. As I discussed remedies for the home and family, including the *ba kua* mirror just mentioned, I felt that the house was laughing at me. Then I noticed that the inset decorative metal pattern in a hole above the gateway of the tunnel entrance (photo pg. 133) and also the doorstep pattern before the front door (photo pg. 147) were special techniques from northern European geomancy to stabilize, shield, protect the home from the T-intersection.

Remember, Feng Shui problems can be solved in a variety of ways and can accommodate individual style and personal background.

A doubled set of Ts with their arms aimed at both the front and the back of a house (4.) is a very bad Feng Shui condition, indicating that the property may become unoccupied or deserted. Unexplainable illnesses or legal problems may beset those who do live there. Ghosts or evil spirits may be attracted. Neighboring houses are easily affected.

A double road that curves away can be difficult to correct. If a road approaches a front door and then curves outward (5.), there may be tendencies toward suicide, lawsuits, or bankruptcy. If the road is like the Chinese character for the figure 8 (6.), two roads moving away from the front door, or, to put it another way, triangulating inward toward your house aimed at the front door, children will not be obedient or amenable to discipline, often clashing with the parents. When they leave home, however, they will have a good development and may treat the parents with kindness. A figure 8-shaped road is bad for one, two, or even more houses. If the shape had nine houses facing it, the bad effect of this formation would be overcome.

If a road facing the house is shaped like a fork with the tines pointed away (7.), both the parents and the succeeding generation will have financial difficulties. Families may be separated. This is the situation of the White House, although Lafayette Park and Pennsylvania Avenue are mitigating factors. In this condition a family may have to sell its properties or

pawn goods to get money. For a nation, the national debt and trade imbalances might grow. Divisions in the nation may be constant.

8.

9.

If the road gets narrower as you leave your home (8.), fortune will decrease and finances worsen. If that road also goes downhill, it will be even worse. If streets run by a house going uphill on both sides (9.), people will feel pressure in family life and have difficulty succeeding. But if roads embrace you, like three Chinese coins, or if you create this condition by construction or landscaping (10.), financial success will be greatly encouraged.

10.

11.

A road like the Chinese figure 7 or a reversed 7 (11.) is very auspicious for wealth. The shape of such a road pattern must be quite straight or balanced to give a feeling of squareness, otherwise, family members will argue. Such a "baked duck" shape (12.) may mean that the family will argue, and that your duck will be cooked.

12.

- **Cul-de-Sacs** have a number of disadvantages in Feng Shui terms. A quiet, peaceful cul–de–sac can be a killing zone in terms of *chi*. The *chi* flows in and circulates, drains the *chi* of many of the homes, and flows out. Its movement, unabated, is too violent and intense to be good for the residence the *chi* flow attacks. The ideal solution is to position an enclosure in the center of the cul–de–sac road in which trees, a fountain, a windmill, or a flagpole are placed. These solutions are also good for traffic circles with spoked turn-off roads. If the shape of the cul-de-sac is square, the houses facing the corners are the worst. Sometimes tenant association rules prevent the Feng Shui correction for the entire group of houses such as adding flags or lighting. In this case, protect your home and its immediate neighbors by attaching a windmill on the roof, a mailbox, or otherwise frontally placed to lift the *chi* of the house and to counteract the draining effect. Sometimes, it is only possible to protect a bedroom. Using tall trees in the back near a bedroom is one good technique.

- **Bridges**. If a bridge gives you a feeling of bringing things to you, of lending a helping hand, it is good. If there is a feeling of pressure, it is not good; a bridge passing above and oppressing a nearby store will harm that store's fortune. If the bridge comes directly at you and faces your property, it may be difficult; if it is parallel to your house, crossing your property, it should be fine. Bridges can be used to link sections of a plot, to connect two ponds, or to otherwise unify and humanize a plot, especially a natural location.

- **Roofs**. Roof shapes are important. In general, if a room has slanted walls because of the roof line, the walls need to be adjusted. A roof ridge pointing at your house can represent a difficult linear impact of *chi* or a quality of pressing down on a house and is not good for offspring or wealth. It may relate to health problems, accidents or unexpected negative events. Typically, a Minor Additions Method such as a *ba kua* mirror is used to reject or diffuse this influence.

- **Churches and Temples** in the immediate vicinity of your home can be good or bad depending on the kinds of activities that primarily occur within. Joyous celebrations like weddings, christenings, Bar or Bas Mitzvahs have a positive influence. A temple specializing in funerals is a difficult influence because of the preponderance of "white," or death, *chi*. Churches or temples are yin, because they are frequently unoccupied. They may be larger than the homes that surround them. Larger structures tend to dominate. For these reasons temples or churches may present Feng Shui problems or benefits.

# THE SHAPE OF THE HOUSE

The guidelines that govern plot shapes also apply to the shapes of houses. The most important thing is to find the balance point for the house or building. Balancing a nonregular shape, attaching an adjusting object, and adding an outstanding feature that regulates the *chi* of the house with the plot and the Earth *chi* are three important techniques.

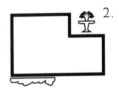

1.

An oddly shaped house (1.), or a house with many protruding or pointed angles, may give the feeling of missing something. One way to resolve this is to add something in front of the house that gives a feeling of balance and encouragement. For example, to an L-shaped house (2.), a spotlight, tree, or pond can be added to create balance. If the shape of the house (or the yard) is not regular, it may hurt the occupants. You may also add vertical flutes in the corners to resolve the irregular shape.

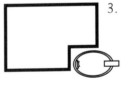

2.

In a boot-shaped house (3.), a pool in the empty area can give a sense of completeness, perhaps with the addition of a "shoelace" of flowers or an extension of vines or ivy to the second story. In this way, additions can adjust for shape, acting, in a sense, as a counterweight. In a boot-shaped house, the area corresponding to the ankle is dominant. If you place your bed or main door on the sole of the boot, you may be stepped on in life. If necessary, a mirror opposite the sole can draw the bed or

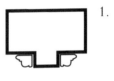

3.

door, symbolically, to the controlling area of the ankle or top of the boot. If the front entrance is already at the top of the boot, and the garage is a projection blocking the view of the street from the front door, you can add either a spotlight beamed up above the front door or add a second path to create balance and equilibrium.

A house shaped like a Chinese lock should not have a master bedroom or a kitchen in the frontal projections. Otherwise the master may feel locked out of that house, frequently sleeping elsewhere or not eating meals at home. Such areas are suitable for guest rooms or offices. A guest who sleeps there will not overstay his or her welcome.

The Chinese cleaver-shaped house should never have a bed or an important desk on the blade edge. People may put pressure on you. If your bed is there, you may have headaches or operations. If your desk is there, you may be fired. To resolve this problem, if you cannot move the bed, put a mirror on the back of the blade and use the Three Secret Reinforcements to draw the bed or desk symbolically into another portion of the shape, like the handle. Otherwise individuals sleeping in this kind of bed may be sick, attacked, criticized by other people, or may even be the victims of fire.

In three dimensional-terms, if the house has a convex shape, you can add flagpoles or lamps to provide symmetry, balance, and to lift the *chi* of that home.

## THE ARRANGEMENT OF ROOMS

The floor plan impacts on the safety and life outcomes of residents. In general, the entry should give a feeling of welcome and encouragement. It should be bright, clear of obstructions, and balanced relative to the house.

Important considerations include the central line and the center line, the suitability of room arrangement for the particular family or enterprise, the position of the Eight Trigrams on the floor plan, and the movement path of the occupants compared to the building's physical structure.

## THE CENTRAL PALACE: YOUR HOME'S CENTER

The central area of the house is the "central palace." The importance in geomancy of the central place, is known in all cultures. An action at the center of a home may affect all areas, influencing the health and energies of the residents. In social, religious, and political terms the center of the city, sacred mountain, temple, palace, or market might serve as the seat of government and the focal point of central authority.

A general idea connected to these aspects of the center is the idea of the vertical center, central axis, or *axis mundi*, connecting Heaven and Earth.

While we have discussed deliberately created centers, the central position of a site is also implicit. In the visual arts is called an "induced structure" not necessarily visually represented but an essential "part of the perceived pattern" with its own emphasis, and psychological and perceptual weight.

Our homes and we, ourselves, are centers and central. The house "imagined as a concentrated being . . . appeals to our consciousness of centrality." As centers of activity, protection, repose, and comfort, the home is analogous to ourselves. Acting from the center can lead to acting for the center. For example, in giving a Feng Shui consultation we borrow the *chi* of the Buddha or our own particular deity and act with that power. In this way we freshly experience a site with less caprice, with fewer "thought-covers," or impositions of habit.

We notice first impressions and special events, combining knowledge of the forms of the Earth and appreciation of the effect of housing situations. The confidence of the center allows such possibilities. Suggesting the center's roots Ranier Maria Rilke wrote:

*Tree always in the center*
*Of all that surrounds it*
*Tree feasting upon*
*Heaven's great dome.*

A kitchen or a bathroom (toilet) should not be in the central palace of the house. If a kitchen is in this central area there may be danger of fires and poor luck. A toilet here may present loss of money, bankruptcy, or tax problems. Mirroring the area, on either side of and behind the stove, will help in the case of a kitchen. Mirroring the exterior of the door to the toilet is the most common method of adjusting for its central position.

## THE INTERIOR CHI ADJUSTMENT

The tai chi position influences all areas. Tai chi is the origin or core of the trigrams. If there are many problems, adjust the tai chi position. One way of doing this is through the *yu nei tai chi* (the interior *chi* adjustment). This is a good method to practice if you've just moved into a seemingly good house and your luck turns bad.

Find the center point of each room. Alternately, visualize the whole house as divided into several squares or rectangles. Some of these may be actual rooms; others may be areas suggested by the layout of the home. Find the center points of these squares or rectangles. Connect these points to determine an area that is called the central area, or the "center of gravity," of the *chi* of the house. To adjust the *chi* of the home, place wind chimes, crystal balls, lights, or plants within the area of all the connected center points. Reinforce with the Three Secret Reinforcements.

You may place the objects of adjustment anywhere in the section you have determined is the heart of the house. For irregularly shaped homes, this area may include a portion that is outside the interior of the house. The rule is that anywhere in the "heart" is suitable if the method of adjustment is appropriate. When asked about this, Professor Lin once jokingly remarked, "When they shoot you, anywhere in the heart is OK."

## THE CENTRAL LINE AND CENTER LINE

The center line refers to the line from front to back along the mid line of the house. The central line refers to the division between the front half and the back half of a house.

The master bedroom, especially, and bedrooms other than guest rooms should be behind the central line. If not, the master may not be able to control the house well. A bedroom located behind the central line is in a more commanding position. One is more able to control the people or the *chi* that comes in from the main entrance. It is all right if a bedroom is on an upper floor, but one should still be aware of the comings and goings in the house. If it is too far removed to have this feeling, add a shopkeeper's bell to the front door or to the door frame above it. Every time the door moves, the bell will ring, alerting the people within and increasing the master's sense of being in control.

A bedroom forward of the central line makes its occupants like doormen.

If the master's bed is forward of the line of the front door, or the *kan* line, it is likely that person will have a bed elsewhere or for other reasons not spend much time sleeping at home. A mirror can be added to symbolically project the bedroom more deeply into the house, positioning it on the interior wall so that the image of the bed is seen as if it were more interior in the home. Placing the master bedroom in the back of the house normally provides quiet, distance from street activities, and the potential for repose. It is like being a general positioned to observe and control an army or like a chief executive whose office is behind his subordinates. It also serves to mitigate dangers of robbery, difficult children or associates, and will lessen possibilities of unfortunate events.

These suggestions about the central line embody the ideas of inner and interior *chi* for the yin and most intimate parts of life and the association of yang activities with the public world.

## INTERNAL STRUCTURES

• **Beams** over a bed or above a desk or other important seating can have a strong negative impact. Lying in such a bed, the area of the body that the beam crosses may suffer an illness or injury. A beam over your legs could lead to leg injuries, car accidents, or block your ability to move forward in life. A beam over your head could produce headaches or other ailments. A beam that crosses above a bed is more severe in its effect than a beam running along the length of the bed. To correct beam problems you may paint the beam the color of the ceiling to make it visually less pressing. Flutes may be placed at 45 degree angles suggesting the *ba kua* or vertically with mouthpiece uppermost. Fake firecrackers can be used to offset the *chi* of the beam with the potential of explosive or uprising force.

- **Ladders and Stairs**. If you open your front door and are met by a staircase aimed toward you, finances may suffer. If the distance from the door to the staircase that directly faces you is less than twice the height of the tallest resident, it needs Feng Shui adjustment. If the staircase is farther away from the door than a person's height, the situation is moderated. A wind chime hung from the ceiling between the door and the staircase is a standard remedy.

Staircases with negative impact include those in the center of a house. Spiral staircases, especially in the center of a house—to put it coarsely—say "screw you!" If you enter a home and see stairs that go up and another adjoining flight going down, these are "Mandarin duck stairs." They are a negative indicator for connubial bliss. If your stairs have treads for stepping on, they should also have risers, the vertical components that connect the treads. With risers, the *chi* can freely move up the stairs. If stairs are narrow, they give the feeling that the amount of food you can eat (which in traditional Chinese society stands for the nourishment you will receive in your life) will be reduced or that your career will get worse.

- **Pillars** can be obstacles if they block your movement. If, for example, at the corner entrance of a business, a pillar blocks you as you leave, it is an indicator that business success will be limited. An open space is understood as yang in quality. The yin quality is increased by many pillars dividing up the space into smaller zones. Generally, round pillars are preferred to square ones. If it is an obstacle, a pillar can be mirrored or covered with artificial vines and flowers to transform it into a tree. The pillar originally was an inverted tree in Egypt. The Ionic, Doric, Corinthian, or Chinese dragon style pillars can be positioned as guardians and protectors of a door. They can elevate the *chi* of an entrance.

- **Doors** are the "mouths of *chi*" for a home or business. Everything about a door is meaningful in Feng Shui. The doors distinguish what is inside and what is outside a room or home. What distinguishes inside or outside the door? Rashi, the famed eleventh-century biblical commentator, called the distinction the *Mashko-of*, or the "banging point." Doors both admit and exclude. They determine what comes in, how it enters, and to a great extent how we will be affected.

The threshold (in Chinese the *kan men*) is very important. Traditional Chinese thresholds are very high and specially measured to assure that ground-dwelling spirits or other bad things cannot enter. A threshold, as the term indicates, has the connotation of keeping in what has been gathered and of not allowing what has been received to depart. As Porphyry noted: "A threshold is a sacred thing." If a threshold has many levels, or irregularities, it indicates that the lives of the residents may have some difficulties.

The front door is called the "big door" in Chinese. It symbolizes the head of a home or office. The door should be clean, fully able to open, and uncluttered. For a large house, a double door may be appropriate for the public front entrance, with lights on either side. (A bedroom should not have a double door.) Even if a side door is larger than the front door, the front door is still considered the primary entryway.

Standing in the main doorway gives you a feeling of the balance of a house from left to right and front to back. In general, a door should open to disclose the wide part of a room. If it does not, rehinge the door so it opens to the wide part of the room. If this is impractical, mirror the wall facing the door opening so you see the rest of the room in the mirror upon entering. You can add an automatic light that comes on when the door opens, or keep fragrant

objects like a bowl of oranges at the entry to adjust the *chi*. If the bedroom is behind the direction of swing of a front door, adding a shopkeeper's bell to that door can avert bad luck, physical danger, or the unpleasant surprises portended by this arrangement.

Sometimes a door will open onto a long narrow corridor that might be along the center line of the building. This is typical of railroad flats or so-called shot-gun flats. If, when you enter, you immediately see out the back, it may be hard to hold onto your money. If the center line corridor has many doors that open onto it, people may be divided against each other. If one person lives there, he may be divided against himself; center line health problems may result. Corridors with many doors are also associated with liver, gallbladder, and spleen problems. Crystals or wind chimes properly placed, along with mirrors to create a sense of wider space, can resolve corridor problems.

If two doors are perfectly aligned with each other, that is completely correct. An exception is a front door aligned with a toilet door or aligned front and rear doors. If doors are completely unaligned, this also is correct. If doors appear aligned but are just barely not, there will be a tendency toward arguments. If doors are slightly unaligned, bickering, criticism, and arguments within the house may be the outcome. If the areas beside misaligned doors are mirrored, the problem is adjusted by creating a sense of balance in the *chi*. In the case of two apartment front doors unaligned, affix a picture of one's child or another appealing image on the wall near the opposite apartment door.

The worst scenario is if the frame of a door coincides with the center of an opposing door. Not only is there an unbalancing effect on the optic nerves, but there will also be a negative effect on behavior, language, emotions, and general health. Nausea or dizziness may result.

If there are three or more doors in a row either aligned or partially aligned, these are "piercing heart" doors. There may be problems with the heart or the center line of the body, headaches, or many conflicting opinions. People may share the same bed but have different dreams. Two crystal balls or two wind chimes aligned with the center line of the door and positioned in the middle of the corridor between the doors can be used to solve this dilemma.

Doors behind you may create heart flutter or nervous system problems. If a big door and a small door are opposite each other, the rule is "big eats small." A big bedroom door and a small bathroom door are just fine. But if the bathroom door were bigger, problems with health, marriage, or money might be indicated.

"Fighting doors" describes the situation of one door physically clashing with another. This kind of arrangement produces arguments or disagreements. People may want to get divorced. One person may want to stay in the house, another may want to leave. If one of the doors is a closet, it may indicate that you have hidden enemies. Sometimes the doors don't actually clash but have that implication. The result may be similar but not as extreme. Employing the three secrets you can resolve fighting doors by placing a red ribbon or cord under your mattress for nine or twenty-seven days. Empower the ribbon to absorb your *chi*, and to be able to represent you energetically. After that time has passed, take the red cord and tie its ends to the knob of each of the clashing doors. Then, cut the cord at its midpoint and wrap the standing ends around each of the knobs, affixing the cord tightly by tying knots, using glue or tape. Empower your action with the intention that those who use these doors will do so in friendliness, or that behind your back criticism will cease.

"Empty doors" describes a situation where there is something like a door frame but no physical door. If the empty door is between a kitchen and a dining room it is completely acceptable. If the empty door is to a bedroom, either husband or wife will tend not to be home. Empty doors may imply affairs outside the home. Perhaps the guardian of an empty bedroom door has lost her mate through death. An empty door should be corrected by adding a physical door, or by adding a curtain, a beaded curtain, or the three–part Japanese curtain called a *noren*. You may, if you like, pull the curtains to the sides. You can also add nine multifaceted spherical glass crystals—four small ones on one side of the door frame, a large one in the center, and four more small ones on the other side. When using curtains or a *noren*, I prefer to also add at least one crystal at the center of the door frame.

It is important to know which door of a room is primary or secondary.

**Secondary doors:**

In *hsun* means your fortune will be lost or you may have tax problems.
In *kun*, partners may not be faithful.
In *tui*, your children are away from home a lot.
In *chyan*, good for patronage.
In *kan*, a good foundation in business.
In *ken*, good for study.
In *chen*, quick development.

• **Skylights**. As a pre-existing feature, a skylight is not considered a problem. Opening a skylight in your home is like cutting into your body, your back, in particular. Opened in an area related to wealth, you might lose your fortune unless you specially handle the installation. An expert can help you choose a day to add a skylight. Otherwise consult Sung's *Almanac*. Using cinnabar and

liquor, draw the outline of the skylight inside the house and visualize as you use the Three Secret Reinforcements that energy and good fortune will be present and increase in the house. Leave the house while the physical installation is being done. Afterward, seal the doors using the procedure described on page 216.

## THE INTANGIBLE DIMENSION

Black Sect Feng Shui emphasizes how to best link action and intention, bringing together tangible and intangible, objective and subjective, physical objects and desire to understand, heal, and bless a home. Important subjective methods include the Three Secret Reinforcements, the Ever-Changing Eight Trigrams, adjusting the external *chi* of the site, and the internal *chi* adjustment; all are described herein.

### PREVIOUS INHABITANTS AND INFLUENCES

Predecessors represent an important invisible influence on a home. Without Feng Shui adjustments, we typically recapitulate the experiences of predecessors because our conditioning is similar to theirs. If there have been negative events, like divorces, demotions, lawsuits, injuries, or deaths, or if a departing family is moving to a smaller house, these may indicate that the next residents may also face unfortunate events. If weddings, promotions, births, and movement to more spacious quarters have previously occurred, these indications are favorable for the new residents. It is very good to know who previously lived in a given location and who now lives there at both material and immaterial levels.

# THE WILD GARDEN

An inhabited house includes both the influence of predecessors and the ancestral background of the occupants. The Romans said, "We bring our lares with us," lares and penates being ancestral and house spirits. The house warming ceremony found in most cultures accommodates the new residents in the spirit of blessing and establishment. If the house spirits and the spirits of the land are satisfied they become protectors and benefactors of the human inhabitants. If they are dissatisfied, while they cannot take us to court, they may find other means to express their lack of comfort. These may include influencing the feeling tone of the environment, producing both trivial and more serious health problems, and affecting the sense of well being and the luck of the residents. Local spirits include the landlord spirit (called by the Tibetans the green *sadag*), soil spirits called *nagas*, tree spirits, and spirits connected with watercourses, hills, kinds of vegetation, or even individual rocks.

The technique of the wild garden creates an area which the local nature spirits can inhabit. In doing so, they will be satisfied and in turn bring great blessings to your own home ground. The wild garden for the spitirts is a created or designated palce where no further human intervention (except perhaps for making offerings) is allowed.

The accommodation of spiritual beings of the site, hearth, or home may be accomplished in many ways, including designating a specific area to belong to the indigenous spirits of the soil, plot, or area. The Thai spirit house, similar to the wild garden, is a miniature model of a human house or temple, like a dollhouse, is one way to fulfill that need in the "wild garden." It is built to accommodate indigenous and designated spirits of the site, plot, or soil where it is positioned. Typically it is built with an odd number of rooms. The Thai spirit house is placed where no shadow of a human dwelling will fall.

## NEIGHBORS

Neighbors know a great deal about each other. If you feel difficulty with a neighbor who lives near you, you could draw a red circle with cinnabar and liquor in the *kan* position or the *hsun* position. Add rice to the mixture and plant nine handfuls of rice, visualizing the power of this blessed mixture descending downward or upward toward that neighbor's home rectifying the problem and bringing both of you into greater harmony. Use the Three Secret Reinforcements.

# THE ARRANGEMENT OF OBJECTS AND THE NATURE OF THE HOME

## NATURAL HIERARCHY AND THE HOME

We can use natural hierarchy of Heaven, human being, and Earth as an aid to understand, plan, and design in Feng Shui. The floor symbolizes the Earth; the walls, the human; and the ceiling, the sky. The natural hierarchy is associated with Confucian learning and has led to thinking of society as a family. We can study and learn to embody the connectedness and unity of Heaven, human being, and Earth, as demonstrated in both the Pillar of the Universe and Standing in the World exercises outlined in Part III.

The sky is above. Heaven is round. The Earth extends to the four directions of the human body (front, back, left, and right) and, thus, is square. Very early in China the idea was that Heaven and Earth were in constant conjugal union. As more and more children were born, the distance between Heaven and Earth increased to make room for all under Heaven. "Ensure harmony in the Middle and Heaven and Earth take their rightful places and all things flourish," says the *Book of Rites*, an ancient text which discusses domestic rites and rituals. This is the domain of Feng Shui.

Heaven is, traditionally the realm of the gods. It is associated with the lofty, vast, infinite dimension that inspires greatness and creativity. The Earth, caring for all things like a mother, symbolizes practicality and receptivity, encouraging and benefiting life.

Where the *chi* of the Earth reaches the surface, the soil will be loose and the Earth can be cultivated. If Heaven and Earth are in right relation, the Earth is pliable and responsive. Rain falls. People combining the freedom of Heaven and the practicality of the Earth (following the exposition of Chogyam Trungpa Rimpoche, one of the most important transmitters of Tibetan Buddhism to the West) will have a sustainable and harmonious culture. If we violate this natural order, we create social chaos and natural disaster. Feng Shui integrates the relationship of Heaven *chi*, human *chi*, and Earth *chi* for harmony in design.

## HEAVEN, HUMAN BEING, AND EARTH OBJECT ARRANGEMENT

We can repair and develop our own connection to the fluency of the Heaven, human being, and Earth natural hierarchy by using a method of object arrangement I learned from Chogyam Trungpa Rimpoche as part of the study of Buddhist aesthetics. You can apply this principle in daily life by choosing three objects and arranging them so that the Heaven, human being, Earth principle is realized aesthetically.

The Earth principle gives support or is a base; the human principle connects; the Heaven principle connects to the universal and cosmic. Perhaps a restaurant table might represent Earth connected by the spoon of human use to the round coffee cup of Heaven. The possibilities are endless and give a dimension of aesthetic training to playing with your food.

# TIBETAN OBJECT ARRANGEMENT

*The world has order and power and richness that can teach you how*
*to conduct your life artfully, with kindness to others and care for yourself.*
—*Chogyam Trungpa Rimpoche*

The Tibetan concepts of *Lha*, *Nyen*, and *Lu* (pronounced as spelled) are functional principles that guide life on Earth, while recognizing the integration of Heaven, human being, and Earth. As Chogyam Trungpa Rimpoche describes them in *Shambhala, The Sacred Path of the Warrior*, these concepts convey "the protocol and decorum of the Earth itself." We can use *Lha*, *Nyen*, and *Lu* to approach harmony with the Earth's "fundamental magic." In this way we put ourselves into a position of strength, or *Drala*, that allows us to connect to basic experiences and elemental qualities and to understand an environment without filters.

Following Trungpa's teaching, *Lha*, literally divine or god like, refers to the highest points on Earth, the peaks of snowy mountains, the point that catches the first light of the rising sun. It is all the places on the Earth and in ourselves that reach into the heavens above, into the clouds. *Lha* is the experience on Earth of greatest closeness to Heaven. It refers to "first wakefulness," freshness of mind, radiance. In our bodies *Lha* is the head, especially the eyes and forehead and represents uprightness, giving, and extending ourselves.

*Nyen* literally means friend. *Nyen* "begins with the great shoulders of the mountain, and includes forests jungles and plains." In the body it is the shoulders, as well as torso, chest, and rib cage. It relates to a grounded courtesy, bravery, and gallantry, "an enlightened version of friendship, being courageous and helpful to others."

*Lu*, literally the water being, refers to the realm of oceans, rivers, great lakes, water and wetness; a rich liquid jewel-like quality. *Lu* in the body is everything below the waist including legs and feet.

*Lha* is winter. Spring is the transition from *Lha* to *Nyen*. Summer is *Nyen* fully developed. Autumn is *Nyen* becoming *Lu*. With *Lu* the fruit is picked and eaten.

In *Lha*, *Nyen*, and *Lu* we have a "developmental process" that can be applied to many levels of experience. Trungpa describes, for example, how these transitions can be applied to natural processes and to the handling of money. As the sun warms a mountain, the snow that begins to melt expresses *Lha*. The running water streams down (*Nyen*) and finally merges with the ocean (*Lu*). Getting money is *Lha*; putting it in the bank is *Nyen*; using the money is *Lu*. In drinking water, pouring it into the glass is *Lha*; lifting the glass is *Nyen*; drinking the water is *Lu*.

We can more clearly see the relationship of these teachings for Feng Shui practice when we apply them to the objects of our lives. Hats, glasses, earrings, hairbrushes, and toothbrushes are in the *Lha* family. Shirts, ties, dresses, belts, watches, cuff links, and trousers are in the *Nyen* category. Socks, underwear, and shoes are connected with *Lu*. Knowing the family of an object enables one to know the proper way to position and relate to that object.

A key point is that if you mix categories, imposing an item from one family in the realm of another, there is a feeling that something is wrong, that "you violate natural hierarchy." Trungpa Rimpoche points to two examples that illustrate this. One is the famous photo of President Kennedy, with his feet up on the desk of the Oval Office. There is a sense of casualness that violates the appropriate order of the prestige of the presidency. The other example is Soviet premier Nikita Khrushchev pounding his shoe at the United Nations podium.

If we follow the order of *Lha*, *Nyen*, and *Lu* our lives can be put into harmony with natural order. If you recognize and apply these principles from inner experience and not as a set of imposed rules, you do not throw your clothes on the floor, leave the dishes on the dining room table, or refuse to put the newspapers in the recycling box. You will participate in the maintenance of order because in this small way you realize your own connectedness to natural process. If you do violate this sense of order, you can take an action to re-establish it. In Judaism, if a prayer book is dropped on the ground, it is picked up and kissed. In Tibet, if a religious text is dropped, it is picked up and held to the forehead to elevate it in respect to the realm of *Lha*.

In Feng Shui consultation, *Lha*, *Nyen*, and *Lu* can be applied. If you enter a home and find garbage or even the smell of garbage near the front door, this is putting a *Lu* dimension factor in the place of *Lha*. If paintings are hung too low, it may be that the *Nyen* dimension of support is being downgraded to the *Lu* position. Rather than elevating and lifting the *chi*, such a painting might have a negative effect. If an object of reverence, like a Buddha, is placed on the ground and there is no corresponding Buddha in a higher position, disrespectful placement may create a sense of imbalance or inappropriateness.

*Lha*, *Nyen*, and *lu* can be guiding principles. To properly sit down to eat with your family, to make your bed after you lie in it, to sit in the commanding position in a workspace that appropriately respects natural hierarchy can contribute greatly to your own unity with the world and to successful Feng Shui.

# THE ARRANGEMENT AND DECORATION OF ROOMS

In the basic doctrine of "suitability," rooms need to be made appropriate for different uses throughout the course of the day, so that daily life is enhanced by their design. This is a classic interior design principle. John Barrington Bayley, in the introduction to Wharton and Codman's *The Decoration of Houses*, remarked that "When suitability departs, every room tends to become a living room." Suitability has a connection with Vitruvius's harmony of "propriety." To emphasize suitability, equitable balance, and the sweetness of life in arranging and decorating an environment is of fundamental importance. Doing so will allow us to say: *Sic Situ laentnatur Lares* ("The household gods delight in being here").

## THE COMMANDING POSITION

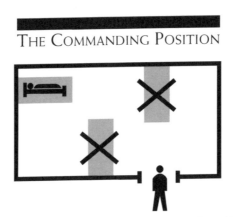

One of the most important principles in Black Sect Feng Shui is the commanding position, a power position that provides a view, prevents surprise, and gives control of an environment. An important application for both interiors and exteriors, the commanding position is a prime example of how Feng Shui helps time work to a person's advantage. Use the commanding position principle for determining the placement of your bed, desk, or other important seating using the following points:

1. Use the relative position (not compass direction) to determine the commanding position. The commanding position is based on the mouth of *chi*, where the *chi* comes in, the primary door of a room.

2. The commanding position should provide a wide viewing area, an open field of vision.

3. The main entrance (the mouth of *chi*) should be within the viewing range of the commanding position, but

4. The commanding position should not face the mouth of *chi* directly.

By being able to observe the mouth of *chi* a person will not be startled or taken unawares. The commanding position for interiors should be toward the back of the room, relative to the primary door. From the commanding position one is able to receive and control what comes in. There is more time to observe and to determine an appropriate response. The wide viewing area assures that everything entering the room can be observed, allows the eyes to relax, and balances personal *chi*. Position yourself so you are not in direct line with the doorway, because the line of force that enters a door can harm your health or your ability to function well. The indirect approach of seeing the door but not aligning with it allows us to receive its *chi* but not be overwhelmed by it.

Early hunting camps of the Paleolithic period used a form of the commanding position principle we call the "comfortable easy armchair." Typical is siting halfway or higher up a hill, with a frontal view of game animals or potential enemies, in a place that provides shelter, concealment, and protection. Classic for Feng Shui is creating a comfortable armchair site for your home, with hill and trees for protection behind like the back of a chair, ridges as arms, and a view to the front, a prototype of the feeling of comfortable control.

## THE FIRST SIGHT UPON ENTERING

## THE FEELING AND TONE OF YOUR HOME

*Houses, like people, have definite personalities and this place is positively ghoulish.*
—*Sherlock Holmes,* Sherlock Holmes
Faces Death

In the practice of Feng Shui, your first impression as you enter a home or room is very important. By crossing a threshold you enter a new environment or another world. You experience particular qualities, moods, and presences, both visible and invisible, that condition our homes and workplaces and influence our lives. For this reason be in a state of unity with Divine Mind and Universal being. Step across the threshold with your left foot if a man, right foot if a woman. Use the dispelling evil mudra and the speech secret from the Three Secret Reinforcements. Open your heart and mind. What do you notice and feel?

Levels of influence begin before we enter. The way we come home or go to work has its significance. If the walkway to the front door is smooth and easy, or difficult, with twists, turns, and blockages, our *chi*, in either case, is affected. Find a creative way, employing methods suggested herein and your own solutions, to make the path to the front door and entrance into the house a positive experience.

When we enter, the first sight that comes into our view and the movement path we follow is significant. Our *chi* is drawn by the first things we see and by how we proceed into the home or workplace. The first sight upon entering principle takes these factors into account and elaborates on their meaning. In the Feng Shui community of knowledge, this unique point of view was developed by Professor Lin. What we see, and where we go, strongly determines the lives we lead. I once asked Professor Lin if we could call this idea "the what you see is what you get" principle. He replied that perhaps this term might not be completely accurate, for otherwise, if it were strictly so, many of us might spend our time hanging out at the bank.

Edith Wharton pointed out that while "the main purpose of a door is to admit, its secondary purpose is to exclude." An entry area, foyer, or vestibule is a transitional place. Ideally it should be spacious, bright, and able to assist the transition from the outer world to the inner sanctum of the home. It should provide a sense of scope, promise, and safety.

Thomas Jefferson had a marvelous sense of the importance of the entry area at Monticello, because he used this space to instruct and enlighten a visitor. A visitor saw a museum of clocks, fossils, paintings of historical subjects, sculptures, maps of the world, and Native American artifacts.

You may hang a metal wind chime or a multifaceted spherical glass crystal from the ceiling in the entry area to encourage clarity, focus, and mental acuity. Place a personally inspiring image, according to your own system of belief, as a spiritual reminder, which you will see as you enter or leave your home to recall and motivate you to your highest purpose.

# FRONT DOOR

If, when you enter the front door, you immediately face a wall that is nearer to you than your own height, you have encountered a "brick wall" situation. Your *chi* is blocked. Hang a mirror on the wall to increase the sense of space and the feeling of being welcome. Have a motion sensor or an electric eye turn on a bright light to increase your sense of space. In this way, the condition of having your progress in life blocked, which can impact your career or health within two to three years at most, will be overcome.

A half wall situation, where at a similar distance one eye stops at a wall and the other eye goes to a distant view, is very unbalancing. It threatens health problems along the center line of the body, harmony between husband and wife, family unity, and mental balance. The near wall is easier to fix because it is the dominant view. One remedy is to mirror the near wall to give a sense of positive reinforcement. In this way one's gaze is attracted to one's own image. Each of us, whatever our self-image, is attracted to our own image. You may also, it is jokingly suggested by Professor Lin, add a picture of your spouse or your former spouse, if you prefer that person more, or alternatively affix nine or ten $100 bills to the wall, so you will count them when you enter to make sure none have been stolen. Adding bright lighting or giving the area the feeling of an arbor, or otherwise adding vitality can also correct this half wall problem.

If, as you enter, there is a glass wall that discloses the kitchen, dining room, or other rooms, the rooms seen will have some effect but not a large effect. In all cases, concentrate on making the entry area bright, spacious, and vital. If you enter through a slanted door, be sure to hang a crystal ball in the entry area to avoid strange or unexpected occurrences or an unusual disease.

## LIVING ROOM

Encountering a living room upon entering provides a feeling of comfort and security and is often a healthy and successful first room to meet. It represents a break from the world of work, a chance for the body to rest and be balanced after the toils of the day. It signifies a change of pace from public activity. Seeing a living room first gives a landing area, a buffer zone between you and the world. You can take a moment to rest, to reflect on what you have done, and to consider what to do next. There is a feeling of restfulness and peacefulness.

## KITCHEN

If when we enter a home we see or are led to our kitchen, there will be a tendency toward digestive, intestinal, and abdominal problems or to weight gain. Sometimes people may become lazy and fat. It is a matter of the eyes seeing and the heart following. Perhaps, in being drawn to the kitchen we will open the refrigerator or eat in an untimely way. Much the same conditioning will be evidenced if you frequently use a back or side entrance that leads to a kitchen.

## BATHROOM

If the first thing we see when we enter a house is a bathroom with a toilet, there will be a tendency to acquire some strange, unusual, or chronic diseases. Once, Professor Lin was a house guest for an extended period in a home in Hong Kong. The first room encountered upon entering was, indeed, a toilet. Upon returning there, after a time, as the professor ascended the steps, he often would begin to feel a certain sense of urgency drawing him to this small room. A restroom that you encounter in this way will affect you, whether you believe it or not. Since you are conditioned toward the restroom, your thinking may be directed to scatological subjects and not to lofty thoughts. If this is the condition of your home, mirror the exterior of the bathroom door.

If a bathroom is first encountered at an office, the workers may gather there to gossip before the workday begins and get a later start each day in their work activities. Adding a mirror to these doors will also be effective. Potted plants or trees, whether real or highly realistic artificial ones, will also help.

## STUDY, DEN, OR LIBRARY

A study or den is very successful and helpful to those who encounter it first because it helps people accumulate knowledge. Perhaps you immediately open your mail, look at the magazines that have arrived, examine correspondence, or do a little research. You will tend to know more than other people and have a wider scope of knowledge and be well versed in current developments. For adults the den or study will assist rapid career development. For children it will advance their studies and help them to have better grades. They will tend to read more. Both children and adults will be more successful. To a lesser extent, the elements of a study or den can be incorporated in any entryway to provide inspiration.

If employees in the workplace first encounter a library or a facility for developing technical skills, their progress and performance will be much enhanced. It's good if the library has glass doors so that workers, seeing others engaged in study, will be encouraged to enter.

# BEDROOM

Bedrooms encountered first may induce a very loose, laid-back lifestyle. People may not be very industrious at work. They may, in fact, be lazy. You may enter and lie down to rest, whether you feel tired or not. Also, a bedroom at the front of a home is not in a controlling position. You may have a tendency to spend time away from home and not sleep in your own bed.

# DINING ROOM

In society today a dining room tends to have mixed functions, but overall it is thought of as an area to eat in. Therefore it has a similar negative connotation as the kitchen. If you encounter a dining room first, hang a crystal ball or wind chime to divert any negative influence.

# CARD ROOM, MAHJONG ROOM, GAMBLING ROOM

Rooms used for gambling may lead to financial ups and downs. Other extreme ups and downs in life or in fortune may be conditioned by such a room.

# THE FLOOR PLAN AND THE ARRANGEMENT OF ROOMS

In examining room arrangement in an overview of Black Sect Feng Shui, we have already touched on the entry, the center line, the central line, the central palace, and the positions of bedroom, kitchen, bathroom, living room, and offices. In terms of the Eight Trigrams, there are some guidelines about the appropriate placement of rooms that supplement these teachings.

If we think of the kind of rooms that correspond with trigram positions, there are some indicated placements. This does not mean it is wrong for rooms to occupy other positions. Conditions of interiorization, or the path of movement, control, and utility, are actually more important as guidelines. But, if it is possible to place it there, a room that corresponds to its optimal trigram position will have an additional element of strength.

## ROOMS CORRESPONDING TO TRIGRAMS

- **Study**: Excellent in the *kan* position. Wisdom will be furthered. The *ken* position, associated with academic work and general skillfulness, is also very suitable.

- **Family Room**: Natural to the *chen* position, which is associated with family life.

- **Child's Bedroom**: Place a child's bedroom in the *tui* position, the area connected with your children and descendants.

- **Kitchen**: The *chen*, *hsun*, *li*, *kun*, or *tui* positions are fine, especially if the kitchen is placed behind the central line of the house.

- **Living room**: Appropriate in the *chyan*, *kan*, or *ken* positions, frontal in the home. *Li*, associated with recognition, is also appropriate for a living room.

- **Guest room**: The *chyan* position is particularly good. It helps make your guests beneficial to you. Its frontal position will help them not overstay their welcome.

- **Center of the House**: Avoid placing kitchens, bathrooms, staircases, fireplaces, or heaters there.

Of course, don't just limit your application of the trigrams to room placement. Remember, when adjusting life issues, to adjust a number of trigram positions. To adjust career, for example, which is associated with the *kan* position, make adjustments in the yard, house, living room, and bedroom.

## THE FRONT DOOR

We have already treated doors in a comprehensive way, but remember that it is the most important element in the home. This finds agreement in the Talmud, the written encyclopedia of oral tradition in Judaism. When asked the question: "What, then, is the significance of 'thy house'?" the answer given is "The way thou enterest. . . ."

## THE KITCHEN

A kitchen properly placed, in design terms, reconciles many factors. For example, placement in the southwest portion of a house might make the kitchen too hot. Proximity to other household work areas, as well as to the garage and family room, is a natural accommodation of a family's movement path and activities. A kitchen may, if there are young children or for security reason, be well served with a view of outdoor or interior areas.

Kitchen design includes the "U," the peninsula, the one-wall configuration, the "L" shape, the corridor layout, and the island. From the standpoint of *chi* and the path of movement, traffic flow and movement blockage need to be considered. Black Sect Feng Shui has a preference for the island type of kitchen, with the stove placed so that the cook stands and works in the commanding position.

The best place for a kitchen may be in the *hsun* or *kun* position of the house. As long as a kitchen is not in the central palace it is all right. Remember, ideally the kitchen should be positioned to the back of the central line. If the kitchen is in the center of the house there is a danger of fire. The money that is made will be easily spent.

# THE STOVE IN RELATION TO
# YOUR LIFE IN THE WORLD

The essence of the kitchen is the range or stove where we cook our food. For most of us the source of our food is our work in the world. In Feng Shui terms, the range and stove are extremely important in their influence on our public life, our career, recognition, and wealth. Keep your stove clean and well appointed. Make sure all the burners work. Use your stove and range; even if you only boil water for tea it will make a difference.

The kitchen or dining room should not be placed outside the *kan* line, or line of the front door. The consequence of doing so is that individuals in that house will eat many meals away from home.

Positioning the stove along the central line but not in the center of the house is very good. People will get along and be in good shape financially. If the stove faces the central palace area but is not in the center, family members will be congenial and get along well together.

From the front door, especially along the center line, if we see the stove, there may be fire or other problems. Add a mirror behind the stove. If you see the stove through two doors from the front door there will still be strong danger of fire or diseases or dangers in which blood will be seen, including nosebleeds, accidents, or operations. If the two doors are only partially aligned, or even unaligned, that is even worse. Tragedies and bloodshed may occur. (My daughter and I went to visit a person very dear to us who had just lost her only grandson in an automobile accident. Her husband had also been killed in a robbery. When we entered the front door, we could see her stove through the unaligned kitchen door.)

If a road faces the stove through the front door this condition may produce many health problems. If there is no door between a living room or a dining room and the kitchen and you can see the stove this is not a problem. However, if from another room you can see the stove, it is not good.

Side doors are not a problem if they do not align directly with the stove. But a side door that does align with the stove may indicate the possibility of blood problems.

If the stove is in direct line with one of the doors of the kitchen this represents a difficulty. If it happens that the stove is in another building, use the doors of that building alone for determining immediate factors of influence. If a stove is positioned behind a doorway, bloodshed, loss of wealth, business problems, or peculiar illness may result.

- A door in the *chyan* position with the stove in the *kun* position may harm a marriage.

- A door in the *kan* position and stove in the *li* position may indicate danger of an operation. But if the door is in the *kan* position and the stove faces the *li* position there is fire danger.

- A door in *ken* and a stove in *hsun* may threaten financial loss or pelvic problems.

- With a stove in the *li* position and the door in either the *ken* or the *chyan* position, there is not the same degree of problem. Doors on either side of a stove indicate problems with money or differing opinions. If you see the stove through two doors, both in the *ken* position, you may need hand surgery.

- A stove in a projection in the *li* position is quite well placed. Reputation may be augmented.

In the case of the door alignment problems that have been described, a principal way of resolving them is to hang a metal wind chime above where you stand when you cook at the stove (below left). Empower this installation to resolve the particular danger that the given situation might create.

## FENG SHUI METHODS TO USE IN THE KITCHEN

Adding mirrors behind and also to the side of the stove can have many Feng Shui advantages. If when cooking food, one is startled, that quality of being startled can enter the food and hurt the entire family. If when standing at the stove your back is to a door, the mirror will disclose anyone entering and also simulate the wide viewing area desirable in a commanding position orientation. If in the mirror, you see the burners of your stove, the burners are doubled or more than doubled in number (below right). More burners, more money is the implication. Use the Three Secret Reinforcements in empowering these mirrors.

# THE BEDROOM

The essence of the bedroom is the bed whose presence defines and predates the function of this room. The bedroom should be behind the central line, where it can gather the *chi* and be in a controlling position.

## THE BED

We typically spend a third of our lives in our beds. The bed should occupy the commanding position based on the relative position of the door, a wide viewing area, having the mouth of *chi* within view and avoiding being in direct line with the main door or with any doors in the room. Sleeping, which is a yin condition, in the mouth of *chi* is much too strong an experience for people to undergo for a long time without adverse consequences.

In terms of trigram positions, a bed in the *hsun* position will benefit wealth. A bed in the *kun* position may improve romantic life. Positioned in both *li* and *kun*, a bed may enhance love and recognition.

If your bed is aligned with a door, hang a wind chime or a crystal ball from the ceiling with a nine-inch red string empowering it to absorb and diffuse any damaging line of force that may impact the body of a sleeper in that bed. If you cannot see the door from your bed, you may suffer from nervousness, irregular heartbeat, or headaches.

If your bed is next to the door, you become a doorkeeper, always wondering what is going on outside, or subconsciously reacting to outside influences in a way that is very unbalancing with potential health consequences, especially along the center line of your body.

If the head of your bed is flush against the same wall that secures the kitchen stove, a person not only may have physical headaches, but be beset by scoundrels and many enemies.

A toilet in a room behind the sleeper's head may cause headaches, brain tumors, or perhaps lead to all that person's money going down the drain. (Even if the toilet is not on the same wall as the bed but in direct line with the bed, there still will be a negative effect.) If you try to resolve this problem by placing a mirror in the bathroom behind the toilet, you will see two toilets. The problem may be even worse. Better to resolve this situation by putting a mirror behind the bed.

You may apply the Eight Trigrams to the bed and use these positions to implement Feng Shui solutions.

## THE RIGHT BED

The bed should be of a type with legs, ideally four legs, so that the *chi* can circulate freely. Futons give a temporary feeling. If you use a captain's bed, be sure that the items in the drawers are appropriate to the functions of sleep—bedclothes and linens, for example; not tools and weapons. It is important that the bed have a headboard that is solidly attached. This has to do with protection and assuring both the possibility of and the stability of relationships.

As for size of the bed, king-size beds have two difficulties. First, as the standard maximum size, the king-size bed implies that the next step may be to move to a single bed; you've already achieved the maximum size. The only direction to go may be downward. The California king-size bed, which is even larger, may correlate with a divorce rate that in the San Francisco Bay area approaches 75 percent. Second, the king-size box spring is usually in two parts, which implies a separation between the partners who sleep in the bed. You can use a red cloth between the box spring and mattress to cover the separation and use the Three Secret Reinforcements intending that the couple sleeping here will be at peace and in harmony.

## MAKING THE BEDROOM A FORTRESS OF COMFORT AND REPOSE

You can make your bedroom a fortress of comfort and repose by using a method called "connecting Heaven and Earth." Attach four red cords (or more for an irregularly shaped bedroom) to the ceiling in the corners of the room so that they extend downward all the way to the floor, definitely touching it. Use the Three Secret Reinforcements with the intent that this method will bring the blessings of Heaven and Earth into the lives of the people who use this room. Think that the cord represents the pillars which hold up an ancient Chinese fortress, thereby transforming your bedroom into a fortress of comfort and repose.

A similar method from Northern European geomancy is to place images of four angels, one in each corner of the walls and ceiling to look down on you and bring divine support and blessing.

### THE LIVING ROOM

An advantage of a frontal living room, beyond the peaceful change of pace, is that the living room has a public function. Living rooms may have either a formal or informal character, depending on whether there is also a family room and to what degree formal entertainment is required. Entertaining visitors without allowing access into the inner or private portions of a home is advantageous. If directly connected to the dining room, the usable area of a living room is increased. Seating is of prime importance. Whether the seating is confrontational, conversational, coordinated, containing separate zones, or designed for integrating larger groups are matters of individual style and design requirements.

## FIREPLACES

Since fireplaces are often part of a living room, their Feng Shui impact is addressed here.

If a fireplace is in:

- **Li:** *Li* relates to Fire; Fire on Fire is all right.

- **Kan:** Water and Fire are destructive to each other.

- **Chen:** In the *chen* position, Wood enhances Fire. A fireplace here is good.

- **Tui:** *Tui* is Metal; Fire destroys Metal. A fireplace here is bad.

- **Ken:** *Ken* is connected with Earth. A fireplace here is all right, but it is a somewhat mediocre position.

- **Chyan:** Fire burns Metal. It might be wise not to use a fireplace here.

- **Kun:** A fireplace in *kun* is OK.

- **Hsun:** A fireplace in *hsun* has mixed reviews. In general, if handled correctly, it is problematic but resolvable.

- **Tai chi:** A fireplace is not suitable in the tai chi position.

To adjust a fireplace in a questionable position, use the Method of Minor Additions. A mirror can be placed behind a fireplace to adjust its *chi* effect. This

will have a kind of cooling effect. Nine plants or nine groups of plants can be placed around a fireplace as a Feng Shui adjustment. They can be positioned as desired: in a straight line, a semicircle, or at different heights. Don't forget the Three Secrets.

Images of dragons, such as statues or paintings, can be used around a fireplace. Green dragons cut down on the fire; red dragons augment the fire.

## THE DINING ROOM

Dining rooms in contemporary culture often fulfill multiple functions. They may serve as the precincts of formal dining but are often collection rooms and fulfill some of the functions of a library or den. The essence of the dining room is the dining room table. When dining rooms first became popular in the West in the eighteenth century, the tables were round or square. The rectangular table, particularly the type that can be extended with leaves, was an English invention. A square or round table is more desirable, because rectangular table tends to separate people. A round table, as is used with a lazy Susan or silent butler in Chinese culture, tends to be more integrating and unifying. The commanding position principle is fully applicable in dining situations.

## THE STUDY OR HOME OFFICE

The home office has grown greatly in cultural importance. It differs from many business locations in that it accommodates fewer people. The basic conditions of the commanding position—frontal placement in a home to connect it with public life and the world outside—and separation from the intimate functions of living are important.

Hang a metal wind chime or a multifaceted spherical glass crystal over where you sit at your desk to encourage successful work and decision making.

## THE DEN

The den (which was discussed in terms of its advantages in a first encounter as you enter the home) can be an inner sanctum for reflection or research. It typically serves as the interface between the home and the world in that it is here that bills are paid, services for the home coordinated, tax records kept, among other things. The den, like the home office, is best associated with the front of the house.

## THE MEDITATION ROOM OR ALTAR

If a room is quiet, bright, nice, and clean, any trigram position is good for a meditation room. The *ken* trigram is especially associated with self-cultivation and would be an especially good location.

For an altar, an interior position of inner *chi* is important. Profound historical conservatism influences my Feng Shui ideas about where an altar should be placed. For at least 40,000 years an inner alcove has been considered the place of highest spiritual vibration and, therefore, most suitable for an altar. While this kind of positioning is ideal, you need not fear placing a divine image in line with the mouth of *chi*, if that is necessary. What is important is that the image that represents Divine Mind or Universal Being should be placed at a fairly high position in the room. If one image is low, make sure that at least another image is placed at shoulder height or higher.

## THE TOILET (OR BATHROOM)

The meaning of the toilet in Feng Shui is certainly influenced by the odiferous and extraordinary public toilets of China. The cleanliness and design of many American toilets are such that they are superior in cleanliness to that of many Third World residences or hotel rooms and sometimes more spacious.

In Feng Shui circles, it sometimes seems there is no good place for a toilet. In Chinese the word for toilet means side room or outside room. One recommended approach is to place the toilet so that it overlaps more than one trigram position. In this way, it is suggested the *chi* will get confused and not be flushed down the drain. The *kun* position is also considered a good place for a toilet. *Kun* represents the Earth, which cares for all things like a mother. So putting a toilet in *kun* allows the Earth to symbolically recycle what is flushed. However, a toilet in the *kun* position may be problematic for some marriages or for those with a tendency toward stomach problems. I recommend employing the Method of Minor Adjustments for toilets in this position. If toilets are on upper floors, use the mouths of *chi* on each floor to determine relative trigram position.

If a toilet is in the *hsun* position, there is the implication that wealth will be flushed away or can quickly leave. Put a mirror on the exterior of the bathroom door or place a Chinese flute straight up and down near the ceiling in the corner near the toilet bowl, mouthpiece uppermost. If the door to the toilet is customarily kept open, you can place a mirror on the wall opposite. You may also affix a small round mirror to the ceiling above the toilet bowl or place a vertical flute in each corner of the bathroom.

A toilet in the *ken* position is not good. A toilet in the *tai chi* position may lead to much money going to the government in taxes. A toilet in the *chen* position is not particularly bad. A toilet in the *li* position can be adjusted by placing a flute above the door horizontally to provide support. If a bathroom is above your head when you enter the house, you will tend to have bad luck and unfortunate occurrences.

## THE GARAGE

The garage tends to be a dominant feature in American housing, often overwhelming the front door. If the position of the garage prevents you from fully seeing the street from the front door, you can place a mirror so you can see the road and all activity in it. Empower the installation so that no opportunities will be lost and your worldly life will prosper.

A special method for a dominant garage is to paint a trompe l'oeil front door on the garage door itself, allowing opportunities and worldly benefit to come to you. Remember to use the Three Secret Reinforcements.

## Rooms above the Garage: Balancing Yin and Yang

A bedroom above a garage can induce anger, arguments, and mental instability. One way of adjusting for this problem is the organic model Method, as discussed in the color section of the Method of Minor Additions. Connect the garage and the room above it as if they together formed a tree. Paint the garage interior brown or retain its natural wood color or add tree limbs. Make the bedroom represent the leaves, flowers, and fruit of the tree. Use the Three Secret Reinforcements with the intention that rather than being drained or harmed by sleeping above the yin space of the garage, the tree of life you have created will lift your *chi* and bring you blessings. If you have no control over the garage, the method will still be effective if you just correct the bedroom.

# FENG SHUI AND THE WORKPLACE

## SITING A BUSINESS

Choosing a good location is the beginning and often the most important element of business success. The *chi* of surrounding businesses and of the neighborhood provide the environment in which your business can develop. Important influences include how neighboring structures relate to a given business in terms of color, shape, height, and signage. What is the dynamic of the area in terms of pedestrian traffic, and vehicular flow? What influences support or weaken the main entrance?

## MOTHER AND DESCENDANT SIDES OF THE STREET

The strongest impetus of *chi* does not necessarily move straight down a street. It often meanders, moving back and forth from one side of the street to the other. However, the general rule is that the higher side of the street, or the side of the street that has the most foot or automobile traffic is the "mother" side of the street and the opposite side of the street is the "son" side. The mother side of the street is considered dominant, more auspicious, better for business, easier to succeed on; the son side is considered subordinate. A taller building tends to lift the *chi* of the Earth. Determining the dominant side of the street is a matter of judging not only the elevation of slope or buildings but also the flow of *chi*. Observe what people do, where people go, how traffic flows.

If a road has shops on either side, business on each side of the street will tend to be different. The *chi* on a street will not be of equal strength on both sides. A place of weak *chi* will make it hard to succeed. Sometimes if one side is improved, the opposite side of the street will tend to worsen. You can add flags on the weaker side of the street to lift the *chi*. If you put up the flags to create an improvement, are you taking success away from your neighbors? It depends. If the businesses are similar you may damage a neighbor's business. If the activities occurring on both sides of the street differ, you very well may add to the *chi* of the entire neighborhood. If a park is across the street from a business and its features are higher than those of the business, the business will find it difficult to develop well. However, there are ways the weaker side can borrow the *chi* of the stronger side.

For example, across the street from a restaurant is a park with a monumental rectangular solid architectural feature that fronts a major arterial road.

Restaurant after restaurant opened in that location and then closed. Finally, one restaurant used a color scheme that emphasized green, brightly accented with strong lights. In this way the restaurant "borrowed" the *chi* of the park and, for years now, has operated successfully.

## CONSIDERATIONS FOR TYPES OF BUSINESSES

If your business is located in a small building you are very much influenced by the roads and by the *chi* and events on the street. If your business is located in a skyscraper, the microenvironment of the building, the individual floor, and the partitions and divisions of the offices is much more significant.

Sometimes a small business can borrow the *chi* of a larger building, like an office or supermarket. A cafe or copy shop can be the access point for customers who occupy the larger building.

## THE WORKPLACE ENVIRONMENT

Important considerations in an office environment are relationship to the door, desk positions, influences of public and private access routes, internal design factors including lighting, color, and room arrangement of principal offices and business functions, cash register position, and divided areas like computer stations.

## The Front Door as an Indicator of Business

A door in the *chyan* position indicates the importance of enlisting benefactors, pleasing the boss, creating relationships that will support the business activity. A *ken* door indicates the importance of application, hard work, handling details, and succeeding through special offers. A *kan* door indicates the need to advertise, involve the public, and the importance of increasing sales through reaching out to potential customers.

## Arrangement of the Workplace

Arranging your working environment includes considering the placement of the office within the building, the placement of the desk and person, ways of using partitions, and the placement of objects like computers.

Nine or fewer desks in an individual office are fine. More desks in an undivided workspace may produce problems for some of the individuals. If desks are too close to a wall, workers may not be industrious. Add a mirror to the wall so the worker will not be lazy. The desks of managers should be separated from workers, ideally occupying different offices.

Persons seated in a doorway or with a door behind them run the risk of being fired or otherwise losing their job. An exit door behind the manager is particularly not good. One individual in this circumstance was advised to change his seat to a superior unoccupied position. Within a few days the person who sat in line with the door forward of where the first individual had been seated was fired.

In offices with many occupants, success is influenced by seating position. If the main door when opened pushes the *chi* to one side, let us say to the right, an individual seated on the right-hand side will be damaged by the intensity of the *chi*. The individual on the left may feel dull and lifeless.

One office should have some extra space to accommodate a widening scope of activity. If it is too crowded it is very difficult to further expand. Similarly it is wise not to make your desk too large for the space it occupies. Otherwise, success and progress are hampered.

Partitions that are taller than the people who occupy the spaces block the *chi*. There is a sense of confinement, a feeling of pressure, an inability to expand thinking. If your back is to the door, if bookshelves block your gaze, or if it is dark, it is even worse. It is better if partitions are low. If they must be higher for sound suppression, then the upper areas can be made of see-through glass. If you must face away from the door, add a rearview mirror. Plants can be used as a unifying element in this kind of office setting, perhaps placed on top of partitions. They can increase the sense of life energy and be empowered to strengthen benevolence and compassion among workers.

## WHERE TO PUT THE CASH REGISTER

The most correct positions for cash registers are in *hsun, kan,* or *chyan*. If a doorway is in direct line with the cash register, place a crystal ball or wind chime between the cash register and the door.

## CORPORATE FENG SHUI

Corporations need the attention Feng Shui gives to the natural world and to people. Feng Shui needs to appreciate the corporate culture, whether authoritarian or socialist, and be able to address the deepest issues in response to what is asked. In helping a corporation succeed, it may be possible to act for a larger goal. If a boss is in an interior corner office, he can create channels of communication between workspaces and his office by creating a pathway convergence, or central hubs, that allow him both access and control.

# PERSONAL CHI ADJUSTMENTS AND BLESSING METHODS

# EXTERNAL PERSONAL CHI ADJUSTMENTS

## THE BA KUA ON FACE AND BODY

One way to examine the *chi* of a person is to overlay the Eight Trigrams on his or her face and examine the face in terms of physical characteristics, including colors, bumps, and scars. Knowing what the elements and trigrams express you can analyze character, know the past, and predict the future. In terms of transitory facial marks, if there is a black spot in the *li* position it may indicate a threat to the person's reputation. The black (Water element color) overcomes the *li* (Fire) position connected with reputation. A red spot in *chen* may mean that family life will thrive; a red spot in *tui* may warn of danger to children.

## THE FIVE ELEMENTS IN PERSONAL DRESS

The colors you wear may express your innate characteristics or the state of your *chi*. You might wear black pants, a blue shirt, and red tie, saying in element color language: Water produces Wood produces Fire. You can wear a black dress, a green necklace, and a red hair ornament. Generally, wear whatever you like, but if you want to emphasize the element colors, use the Three Secret Reinforcements to empower your appearance.

You may choose to emphasize a particular element to correct something missing. You can wear all five colors in order to express the hope of understanding all five virtues connected with the elements.

## Using the Five Elements with People

To adjust someone else's *chi*, you must adjust your *chi* first. As in Feng Shui, you must evaluate *chi* using the Five Elements. Based on your element knowledge, you will be able to make proper adjustments. Against selfishness be stubborn. Against stubbornness be cutting. Against cruel words use reason, spirit, and stature. Be wise with the angry, not selfish. For the ignorant be trustworthy. These choices are only examples. Of course, each situation has its own requirements.

Remember that the range between extreme talkativeness and choked silence is the domain of the *chi* of Metal. The range between swallowed anger and its intemperate expression is the domain of the *chi* of Fire. The range between flexibility and stubbornness is *chi* of Wood expressed. The balance between selfishness and selflessness is the *chi* of Earth. Social activity and wisdom are the realms of the *chi* of moving and still Water.

## THE VIRTUES OF THE ELEMENTS

Remember, Wood is connected to kindness; Fire, to propriety; Earth, to reliability; Metal, to righteousness; and Water, to wisdom.

Applying the production order we can see that righteousness (Metal) creates wisdom (Water). Wisdom may lead to human heartedness (Wood). Human heartedness leads to courtesy (Fire). Courtesy helps create trustworthiness (Earth). Trustworthiness encourages righteousness (Metal).

In terms of the overcoming sequence, self-righteousness (Metal) overcomes human heartedness (Wood). Excessive stubbornness (Wood) overcomes trustworthiness (Earth). Untrustworthiness (Earth) is unwise (Water). Ignorance and stupidity (Water) develop anger (Fire). Unbridled anger (Fire) overcomes even righteousness (Metal).

## NEGOTIATING WITH PEOPLE USING THE FIVE ELEMENTS

When you want to change another's *chi* using the elements, it is good to evaluate yourself first. What is my own color? What element do I enhance? What element enhances me? If I am Fire, I enhance Earth; I am enhanced by Wood. These three aspects are often used in Black Sect Feng Shui solutions.

We can also investigate: What is my original color? What destroys me? What do I destroy? Some people, when going out to negotiate, wear two colors that are visible, but carry three other element colors hidden on their persons, for example, handkerchiefs or scarves. Thinking what may destroy the element color of the other, they may use the appropriate color as a means of influencing the *chi* of the negotiating partner. If two people wear red, their discussion may grow louder and louder in argument. If one wears red and the second wears green, the second may enhance the first.

## INTERNAL PERSONAL CHI ADJUSTMENTS

### CALMING THE HEART FOR CALMNESS, CLARITY, AND UNITY WITH THE UNIVERSAL

The calming heart method, a profound and simple meditation, is based on the mantra that epitomizes a thousand years of Indian Perfection of Wisdom

teachings. This method draws upon a vast teaching and puts it in a nutshell so we can calm our hearts and minds. It is good to practice first thing in the morning, just before sleep, or at any time you wish to pacify your mind, calm down, or connect with your own inherent universal nature. Use this Meditation to begin any other meditation or method; whenever you are emotionally upset or unclear, as a preparation to use the Three Secret Reinforcements for empowering a Feng Shui installation. (I have seen this method tested in the extremes of life. My father, dying of cancer, used the heart calming method instead of morphine.)

- Begin the calming heart mehtod in the quiet heart hand position, known also as the *dhyani*, or meditation mudra: Place your left hand on top of your right hand, palms up, thumbs touching, in front of your chest as if you were cradling your heart center.

- Recite the heart calming mantra. The words are: GATE GATE PARA-GATE PARA SAM GATE BODHI SVAHA (pronounced *Gah Tay Gah Tay, Pahra Gah Tay, Pahra Sahm Gat Tay Bode-ee Svah Ha*). The words could be translated literally as follows: GATE, *gone;* GATE, *gone;* PARAGATE, *gone across;* PARA SAM GATE, *completely gone across;* BODHI, *the Enlightened State;* SVAHA, *it is accomplished, I recognize this truth in myself.*

- Intend that your heart and mind grow calm and peaceful and that you fully connect with your own intrinsic unity with the Divine Mind.

The meditation is threefold: Hold the mudra; chant the mantra; express the intention. Repeat this process nine times to calm your heart.

## THE INHALE-EXHALE METHOD FOR PURIFICATION

The inhale-exhale method is a powerful simple meditative exercise for purification. You may practice while still in bed upon awakening after the heart calming method. Although you can practice while sitting, lying, or standing, learn it first while standing

• Practice the heart calming method (use one round of nine repetitions or three rounds of twenty-seven total repetitions).

• Inhale deeply, taking a full breath in through your mouth. You are breathing in fresh clean air. With experience, add the visualization that you are breathing in natural light, like sunlight or moonlight. You may also visualize you are breathing in spiritual light, like the light of Buddha or the light of your own primary deity. You may have the feeling of breathing in sound; for example, the mantra *Om Ma Ni Pad Me Hum*.

As we inhale, our lungs expand. Let the air, light, heat, or sound reach below your belly button to the *tan tien*, (the "big gall" or "red field") two or three inches below the belly button, and, dividing the body front to back into ten parts, about three parts inward from your belly. Allow the light to fill your whole body from head to toe, allowing the body to expand with the breath. Fully taking in positive *chi* with your inhalation, allow the breath and light that now fills your body to absorb all *chi* of anger that you either swallowed or intemperately expressed—all unhealthy *chi*, negative Karma, the *chi* of grievances, frustrations, ill-health *chi*, inauspicious *chi*, unlucky *chi*, or the feeling of having done wrong.

- Exhale through your mouth in nine portions, eight short puffs and one final prolonged exhalation. Breathe out all negative factors and visualize them leaving your body as black smoke. It is generally best to exhale gently, feeling the negative qualities, and accepting negative beliefs, tensions, or emotions fully even with love. Then gently exhale. But if the emotional shock is strong (perhaps you've been in an argument with a loved one and don't want to continue in this way) you may wish to use some force in the nine exhalations.

Visualize as you inhale that an infinite number of your cells are activated and respond and that your mind and spiritual powers improve. When you exhale, visualize that all suppressed *chi* is coming out and you are freed of its influence.

- Reinforce the inhale-exhale method with the Three Secret Reinforcements, visualizing you have completely purified yourself of all obstacles.

The inhale-exhale method improves health. In particular, the throat, bronchial tract, heart, lungs, stomach, and intestines are strengthened. Good luck, mental ability, and spiritual power are enhanced. Martial arts practice is benefited. One's mental state or mood is improved. If a person has choked *chi*, bad luck, too much or too little of the *chi* of the Fire element, or is under excessive social strain in terms of economics, peer or family pressure, work or political situation, or has a tendency toward unusual ailments or mental problems, or whose *chi* is generally weak, the inhale-exhale method is very useful. Those who are taciturn, lose opportunities, or complain about their misfortunes will also benefit.

The inhale-exhale method is usually combined with the six-stage chi improvement method. First practice the heart calming and the inhale-exhale method. Then practice the six-stage *chi* improvement method.

# THE SIX-STAGE CHI IMPROVEMENT METHOD

The six-stage *chi* improvement method is among the most important Black Sect methods for developing intuition, spiritual growth, and good health.

- First, calm your heart and practice the inhale-exhale method.

- Now, visualize your body as segmented into six sections. The first segment is from your soles to your knees. The second segment is from your knees to the bottom of the hipbone. The third segment is from the hips to your waist. The fourth segment is from the waist to the throat. The fifth segment is from the throat to the "third eye," the middle of the forehead. The sixth segment is from the third eye to the crown of your head.

- Having divided your body mentally in this way, take in a long deep breath and visualize that a white ball of light enters your soles and that the area from the soles to the knees is completely filled with glowing white light. The light makes the sound OM, and it vibrates throughout this segment of your body. Continuing the inhalation, visualize that the *chi* continues to move upward through the segments of the body, from knee to hip, from hip to waist, from waist to throat, from throat to third eye, from third eye to crown. Each time the chi enters a new segment of your body, its color and sound changes.

The process of inhalation in six stages is as follows:

1. OM, from soles to knees; white;
2. MA, from knees to hips; red;

3. NI, from hips to *tan tien*; yellow;

4. PAD, from *tan tien* to throat; green;

5. ME, from throat to third eye; blue;

6. HUM, from third eye to crown; black.

As you visualize each segment and inhale, emphasize inwardly seeing the color and hearing the sound. You may divide the inhalation into six segments when you begin to practice this method. Later, with experience, one continuous inhalation will correspond with visualizing color and sound rising through the six segments of your body.

• When you exhale, visualize that a geyser or fountain of black light vigorously rises from your crown high into sky above and that all negative *chi* exits from the crown of your head and that you are completely filled with auspicious *chi*.

This method allows the *chi* to flow through your body with ease. Health, wisdom, luck, and sensitivity are improved. This method improves one's outlook on life, generally. It helps in cases of chronic or mental illness. It improves patience and helps accumulate good karma and develop generosity.

## THE PILLAR OF THE UNIVERSE, OR STANDING IN THE WORLD

The Pillar of the Universe, or Standing in the World, is the profound gift of Sifu Kuo Lien Ying, my root *tai chi* chuan master. With this way to stand we build into our body and understanding the dynamic experience of Heaven, human being, and Earth. The process helps you develop, gather, and conserve *chi*. It makes you a Feng Shui "compass." It allows you to tap the *chi* of a natural location and gather it in your own body. It can teach you to study your body as a site "to see the whole spatio-temporal world as mirrored in the bodily life," as twentieth–century American philosopher Alfred North Whitehead phrased it.

The Pillar of the Universe is a standing meditation. It is a method of stillness, personal attunement, and of approach to Emptiness, as well as a means of developing the will. It is a method of *chi* cultivation, a form of *chi kung*, which allows us to study the human body in its energy aspect. The meditation is a method of meeting with place, studying place, and gathering the vital energy of a location with strong and positive *chi*.

This unusual exercise develops mental health while gradually promoting physical strength. It is most effective to use this method after strenuous exercise or at a time when your *chi* is flowing.

Standing in the Pillar of the Universe position is based on circles and squares. Heaven and Earth mediated by human being is the principle at play. The arms are held in a big circle which corresponds to Heaven. The feet are placed in a stance that suggests a square, which corresponds to Earth. The spine and back are kept vertical and straight.

In Pillar of the Universe you alternate corresponding leg and arm positions. You therefore stand for a given time with 90 percent or more of your weight resting on your back foot. Then switch your left and right arms and feet and repeat the exercise for about the same time to fully balance and integrate your *chi*.

Begin by standing straight with head up. Feet are parallel, with weight equally distributed, shoulder width apart. Look far away, ideally at a tree or a beautiful distant prospect. Then move one foot forward, so that the ball of the forward foot rests on the ground and the heel of the forward foot is raised relative to the ball of the foot at an angle to the ground of 30 degrees. The feet should be at an angle of 60 degrees to each other and almost all the weight should be on the rear foot. If the feet are placed too narrowly or too widely, circulation of *chi* will not be optimized.

Slowly raise your arms to make a big circle. Wrists, elbows, and shoulders are all at the same height. The shoulders are relaxed, drawn downward, and sunk. The hands never go below the navel or above the eyes. The forward hand is about two inches in front of the rear hand. The distance between the fingertips of each hand is between four and six inches. The hand associated with the front foot is slightly more forward than is the hand on the same side of the body as the rear foot that bears your weight. The fingers are slightly separated. The opening between thumb and pointer, called the "tiger's mouth," is wide. Feel as if you were holding a 30-pound steel ball in your hands or as if you are holding the full moon in your arms.

The method of practice is to continue to hold this posture for a time. Outwardly you appear to be still; internally there may be great movement of your *chi*. After a time (for some people just a few minutes) it may become difficult to maintain this posture. You could quit, stopping the exercise. You could continue by straining. You could continue by maintaining the correct position and by opening the knots of the body by relaxing and allowing the flow of *chi* to support what otherwise might be a difficult practice to maintain. This last approach, to open by softening, to accept some difficulty and continue by opening, relaxing, and softening the body, is the recommended method of practice.

Pillar of the Universe is one of the great gifts we can give ourselves. Success depends on your own efforts. The posture requires you to stand up properly and to remain in equilibrium. Distinguish between the hollow and solid aspects of your body in terms of weight bearing. Spread your arms in a ring as if embracing someone. Breathe freely and naturally. Have the feeling your head is pushing upward, but use no force. Keep your legs neither tightened nor bent. Release the muscles throughout your body and allow total free circulation of blood and *chi*. You will feel the *chi* sinking to the *tan tien*, the knees rising, the heels twisting outward, the hair standing up on end, and the whole body beaming with light.

The practice method should be to take the entire body as a unified system and soften, soften, soften the physical body and the mind but continue standing. If your mind is agitated you may observe the natural distant view you have chosen. You may allow tension to flow downward through the rear leg into the ground using your breath, sinking into the Earth. Your standing should have a dynamic quality. When I first met Sifu Kuo, he pointed to a tree and indicated that I should practice the Pillar of the Universe not only facing a tree but standing like a tree. This is one way to practice the standing with vitality, inner movement, and outer stillness.

If your mind continues to be agitated, you may sway back and forth, shifting your weight from back to front and from front to back for a moment. If you need to you may walk around in a small circle, and then return to the proper standing posture. Do not lower your arms or your eyes while walking.

If you cannot stand for an hour a day, half an hour on each side, you are still taking what is called the "test of laziness." There will come a time during standing when your hands feel extremely hot almost as if they were burning. This is called the "test of fire." It may last for a month or two. This may be followed after about a year with the "test of water" during which time your hands will feel very cold.

The ultimate aim of Pillar of the Universe is to gather strength without effort and to experience unified energy and peace of mind. There is a sense in which the whole universe is at your fingertips and that you are standing in the center of the world. The Pillar of the Universe allows us to increase faith in our efforts, and to develop patience and perseverance. Sifu Kuo has described this exercise, saying: "Creation will take the place of torture." He wrote the following poem about this method of standing:

> *Boxing, yet no boxing*
> *Meaning, and yet no meaning.*
> *Within the midst of meaningfulness, the true meaning.*
> *Speaking of truth, knows no truth*
> *To cultivate this Way is to leave the body of toil.*

To stand at a "dragon's lair" or another place where the *chi* of the Earth is abundant can allow one to absorb it in one's body, integrate with it through breathing, and achieve identity with the site. By standing like a site you know where you stand. Studied in stillness, a natural location resumes its functioning after about fifteen minutes. The Pillar of the Universe, which makes of the human body the equivalent of the Feng Shui compass, is the perfect viewing platform for Feng Shui investigation.

# THE EXTERNAL ADJUSTMENT
# OF THE CHI OF THE SITE

## BLESSING METHODS

We all must address those mundane issues that are integral to a situation. It is vital to address the visible, objective, and tangible dimension as well as the invisible, subjective, and not ordinarily visible. In Black Sect Feng Shui blessings are emphasized more than in other traditions but all traditions of geomantic knowledge give site blessings great importance. Even if all visible dimension suggestions are not followed, if the blessings are very strong a positive outcome is most likely. In Black Sect Feng Shui it may not be necessary to even provide a visible solution. Using the intangible power of blessing methods to adjust Feng Shui marks a primary distinction between the Black Sect and other Feng Shui schools.

Blessing methods adjust the *chi* of place, home or person. They are among the most important parts of a Feng Shui consultation. Blessing methods to adjust the external *chi* of the site may be used for a home or business, at the time of demolition, ground breaking, laying a foundation, upon moving into a new home or workplace, or at a wedding.

A mixture of rice, cinnabar, and high-proof liquor is prepared (see below). The mixture is then used in three separate stages at the site. The first use of the mixture dispels negative energy. Following this, you plant seeds of productive *chi*. This is termed "planting lucky fields." Finally, the mixture is used to make the *chi* be more rising and joyous, creating a rain of delight and blessing.

1. **Personal Preparation.** Practice the heart calming method, the inhale-exhale method, and the six-stage *chi* improvement method. In your own way come into perfect unity with Divine Mind and Universal Being. You may visualize that your *chi* dives into the Buddha of your heart, meaning your own root deity whatever you conceive it to be, and brings that *chi* back into your own body. Have the feeling that you now have the Buddha's supreme wisdom, compassion, appearance and qualities. Allow your unity with the Buddha to guide you in performing the ceremony of adjusting the *chi* of the site.

2. **Preparing the Mixture.** Place uncooked rice in a bowl. (Remember, rice represents nourishing *chi* but also symbolizes all the Five Grains associated with the Five Elements). Fill the bowl at least halfway. Gauge how much rice will be needed in terms of the size of the space to be adjusted. Add a packet of cinnabar powder, placing it on top of the rice. The minimum amount of cinnabar to use is about a quarter teaspoon. (Cinnabar is sulfide of mercury, called *Ju-Sha* in Chinese, meaning literally red sand. In Buddhist thought it is associated with realizing the activities of power and protection. It can be purchased in Chinese pharmacies.) Add nine drops, pours, or capfuls of high-proof liquor or distilled spirits to the bowl. (Liquor often called "spirits" is thought to have a vibrational level in its speed of evaporation that matches and can overcome the vibrational speed of noncorporeal spirits.) Eighty proof is the recommended minimum concentration, but 151-proof rum is even better. The size of the drops of liquor should be such that the liquor, cinnabar, and rice when stirred will form an even mixture that is slightly moist. Stir the mixture with your middle finger. The middle finger represents oneself. Used this way the finger symbolizes a *vajra*, or thunderbolt. As you stir the mixture repeat either 10 mantras or sacred prayers 9 times each or

repeat the mantra OM MA NI PAD ME HUM 108 times. In this way the power of the prayers and your intention to energize the mixture enters the rice.

3. **Practicing the external chi adjustment.** This blessing method may be performed in a variety of ways. You may walk around the perimeter of a building, around the block on which the building is placed, perform all stages of the blessing while standing in front of the building, or even practice this method indoors. In moving around a building you may walk either in a clockwise or counterclockwise direction.

 **a. Dispelling Evil.** Grab a handful of rice and sprinkle it outward with your palm up. This is the giving mudra. Have the intention that you are offering this blessed rice to feed the hungry ghosts or roaming spirits that might create disturbance and to remedy any negative factors that may block positive development. You may throw the rice to the four cardinal directions or to the front, back, and sides of the lot. In a ground-breaking ceremony, offer the rice in this way a total of nine times, visualizing that the mixture covers the entire site.

 **b. Planting auspicious chi  or planting lucky fields.** Throw handfuls of rice with palm downward. This gesture is called the "seeding mudra" and symbolizes sowing seeds of blessedness into the ground. Throw the rice downward to the four directions, visualizing that the blessing fills the property and extends outward without limit into the world. In a ground-breaking ceremony throw nine handfuls of rice in this way.

 **c. Elevating the chi.** Finally, throw three handfuls of rice high into the air. This helps make the *chi* rise and creates, as the rice falls down-

ward, a symbolic rain of delight and blessing. Have the intention that the home or workplace will be blessed, that the residents or workers will be happy, healthy, and make progress, and that the total enterprise will be completely successful. In a ground breaking, when you throw the rice upward the first time, visualize that the future will be very positive. In throwing the rice upward a second time, visualize that the immediate environment will be peaceful. Throwing the rice upward the third time, visualize a general blessing for peace on Earth and the liberation of all beings.

## SEALING THE DOORS

Sealing the doors is recommended when there have been problems with predecessors in a home or business. It is a protection against difficulties that may be threatened from the outside—robberies, mud slides, water problems—or evil happenings the result of voodoo or magic or an evil encounter that could follow you home.

### THE PROCESS

Use realgar (arsenic sulfide), or *shiung huang* in Chinese, obtainable from a Chinese physician. Realgar in Arabic means the stuff from the mine. This substance is poisonous and therefore should not be ingested. Spiritually, realgar emphasizes the prophylactic power of sulfur.

Combine one teaspoon of realgar and nine drops of high-proof liquor in a bowl to make what will be a thick paint. Stir the mixture with your middle finger, repeating OM MA NI PAD ME HUM 108 times. Then with the middle finger dip into the mixture and touch the positions on the front door, all external doors, including the garage door and the door of the master bedroom and other bedrooms from within the house or room. After dotting the doors, flick some of the mixture upward using the dispelling evil gesture in the centers of each room. Also dot the burners of the stove, the legs of each bed, important desks or tables. Dot important chairs on the underside of the seat. Finally, add some water to the remaining mixture and pour some of the mixture down each drain in the house or wherever water may exit, including sinks, washing machine, toilets, and dishwashers.

Perform sealing the doors on an auspicious day or in the 11 A.M. to 1 P.M. time period, or alternatively from 11 P.M. to 1 A.M. Traditionally doors are sealed once a year on the fifth day of the fifth month of the Chinese lunar calendar.

As you dot each position, or flick the paint upward, visualize that all negative *chi* is removed, that no negative *chi* can enter, and that the environment is filled with buoyant positive *chi* and blessings. Reinforce each action using this paint with the Three Secret Reinforcements. Conclude with nine repetitions of the Three Secrets. Visualize that the process of sealing the doors has been completely effective.

- You can seal the doors of a car; in this case touch the bumpers and tires.

- If there is a health problem that relates to a part of the body that needs fixing, either before reconstruction or just after the problem is repaired, seal the doors. If you have the ability to judge that this is a case of a murder at those premises or a severe run of bad luck, seal the doors.

- If you have been away from your home for a long time or only occupy a home for a short time each year, when you arrive to occupy that home, seal the doors.

- If doors have been blocked, or if your bedroom is outside the line of the front door, as in the case of a Chinese lock-shaped house, seal the doors.

## REMOVING BAD CHI: BURNING CHEN PI

Sometimes an environment suffers from difficult invisible influences.

These can be of many types ranging from the residue of predecessors' lifestyles, the energy of horrific events, draining yin *chi*, a feeling of evil, or the presence of actual entities. In such cases, the *chen pi* purification can create dramatic improvement.

The purification is carried out using both fresh orange peel and aged dried tangerine skin, called *chen pi*, which is available in both Chinese medicine and food stores. This method is comparable to the Native American practice of smudging with sage but, most of the time, it is even more effective.

1. **Preparation of the plate.** Cut nine round pieces of fresh orange peel and use nine pieces of *chen pi*. Place all the pieces on a white plate. You may place the orange peel and *chen pi* in a variety of patterns.

2. **Carrying out the chen pi purification.** Starting at the front door, light the pieces of *chen pi* one by one as you walk clockwise throughout

the space, saying the mantra OM MA NI PAD ME HUM. (A cigarette lighter works more efficiently than matches.) Visualize that the smoke of the burning *chen pi* and the power of your utterance drives out all bad *chi*. Walk through all the stories of the building (or in a very large building all the space belonging to the family or business to be helped). As you move through the space, light successive pieces of *chen pi*, spacing the process so that all nine pieces have been lit by the time you complete your progress. If the space is very small, you need not light all nine pieces. If the space is very large, you may relight pieces of *chen pi* that have ceased to produce smoke.

3. **Conclusion of the chen pi purification.** Continue walking through the space in a clockwise manner until you return to the front door. Then walk with the plate to the stove and place the plate on the center of the range or on one of the burners. (Do not turn the burner on.) Complete the purification using the Three Secret Reinforcements, visualizing that this site purification has been completely successful. Allow the plate to remain on the range top overnight. In the morning, dispose of the *chen pi* and orange peels, throwing them away without ceremony.

Some extraordinary results occur in conducting this purification. I once had the occasion to consult in what had been the home of Meriwether Lewis in Charlottesville, Virginia. I could feel a strongly difficult *chi* in the basement. In using the *chen pi* purification, I first prepared the upper floors. Then, as I and an apprentice began to descend the basement stairs, there was a huge rush of something like wind that made papers fly in the air, and almost knocked over my rather sizable assistant. The difficult *chi*, however, escaped into an environment that had been prepared for it and was forced to leave the home completely.

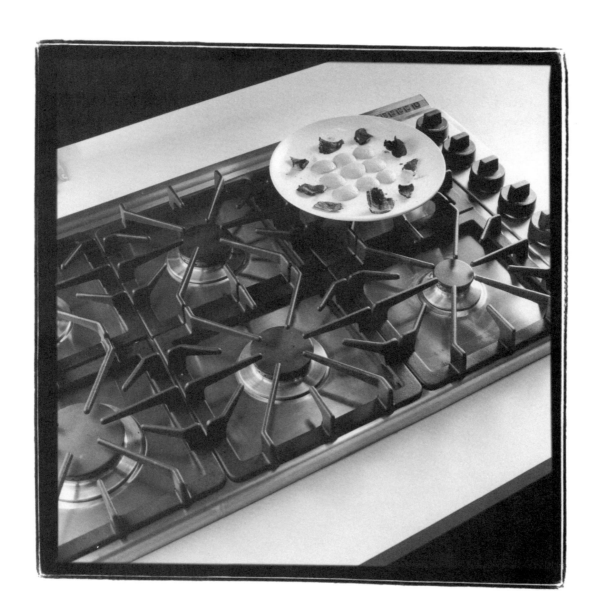

# MONEY SECRETS OF FENG SHUI

Monetary issues are among the prime reasons Feng Shui experts are consulted. Black Sect Feng Shui has an abundance of methods to improve finances. Among the important Feng Shui site indicators of difficulty with money are:

- A site that is wide but not deep;

- A plot or house with a "dustbin" rather than a "money bag" shape;

- Stairs that are near to and directly face the front door;

- Seeing through the house to the outside when you enter;

- Missing portions of the home in terms of the overlay of the Eight Trigrams;

- Roads that have problematic directions, curves, or forks or can't be seen.

It is said in China that money has two spears. The misuse of money is a spear that can hurt your character. The lack of money is a spear that has prevented many people from fulfilling their mission in life. Indeed the word for poverty includes the pictograph for cave or hole. To be "in the hole," in this sense, is an experience that has buried many heroes.

If you have money, you are held to be able to speak with the deities; ghosts will help you turn the millstone of your fate. Water is associated with money. Just as water can give life to plants, we also must drink water to live.

Like water, money is necessary to live. It is not enough just to have money; we must learn to use it properly. As with water, money can safely transport us on the boat of life from port to port. But money misused can make the boat of life overturn.

Money is unique in that its marginal utility does not decrease when we have more of it. For a thirsty person, a glass of water may be gratefully received. A second glass may be welcome. But the value of the tenth glass of water is not the same to a person whose thirst has been sated as was the first. This principle of diminishing marginal returns does not apply in this way to money. I once gave the piggy bank method I am about to describe to a multi-millionaire hotelier. He readily undertook the practice because, even though to the eyes of the world he would be recognized as extremely wealthy, he had a particular purpose to achieve that made him want even more money.

## THE GREAT WEALTH ACCUMULATOR, PRECIOUS TREASURE BOX, OR PIGGY BANK METHOD

This special method both attracts cash and imparts valuable lessons about money. The treasure box you create and in which you place money is the symbolic root of your wealth. It is like a mother who will have many children—meaning, much more money.

You need the following materials to practice the great wealth accumulator method:

- A piggy bank or other container to store money in, of a size to fit under your bed;

- A new pen with black ink bought especially to use for this purpose;

- A red paper, round or square, about three inches on a side to be used as a label for your piggy bank;

- A square red cloth larger in size than your bank, to be used as a base piece to keep the bank off the ground;

- Two round one-sided mirrors approximately three inches in diameter.

The procedure for the great wealth accumulator method is:

1. Practice the heart calming meditation on an auspicious day or at least during the 11 A.M. to 1 P.M. time period.

2. Deeply inhale. While holding your breath, write GREAT WEALTH ACCUMULATOR on one side of the red paper label and sign your own name on the opposite side of the paper.

3. Attach the label with tape or glue to the piggy bank with your name hidden on the inside facing the bank.

4. Place the red cloth on the floor under the bed directly under where your primary hand (usually the right hand) would rest when you are lying on the bed with your hands slightly extended outward near your side.

5. Place one of the round mirrors on the cloth, mirrored surface facing the ceiling.

6. Place the bank on top of the mirror on the red cloth. The bank should rest partly under the bed and be partly exposed next to the bed.

7. Attach the second round mirror to the frame of the bed above the piggy bank, mirrored surface facing downward.

8. The piggy bank has now been prepared for accumulating wealth.

9. Use the Three Secret Reinforcements to empower the piggy bank.

10. Choose a particular denomination of coin that you will collect and place in the piggy bank. (Alternatively you may choose to collect all coins that you receive or to designate a particular denomination of bill to collect.)

11. Every day for twenty-seven consecutive days, collect at least one coin of the chosen denomination and place it in the piggy bank. All the coins of that denomination that come into your hands must be collected and placed in the bank. No coins of the chosen denomination may be spent. Place all the coins in a particular pocket or have a special coin purse for them. Separate them from your other money.

12. Place the collected coins in the piggy bank when you return home from work, before going to bed, or before midnight of that day.

13. After placing coins in the bank each day, reinforce this action with the Three Secret Reinforcements.

14. After completing the cycle of depositing coins in the bank, you may either leave the piggy bank in its place at the side of the bed or place it in the *hsun* (Wealth) position of your bedroom.

Your objective in carrying out this method is not necessarily to fill up the bank but to create a collection of money that serves as a money magnet. The experience of special methods changes us as we carry them out. During the process of collecting the coin, for example, you may need to visit stores to get coins of the designated denomination. Perhaps you have run across a busy street rushing to avoid oncoming traffic. You enter the store and ask for change of a dollar. The storekeeper, however, refuses, saying you must buy something to get change. You may learn from this experience about how hard it is to acquire even a quarter. Your understanding of money may reflect a different attitude about the uses, function, and value of money. In this way you may become more careful not to waste money. Having created the root of wealth in the piggy bank, your sensibility may change from regarding yourself as someone who does not have money to someone who has a special treasure. In these kinds of ways your perspective, theories, and knowledge about money may change. This is an example about one of the ways a transcendental cure operates.

In using the Three Secret Reinforcements visualize that wealth is pouring into your piggy bank after being collected in your hand. The mirrors intensify the strength of the method but are not absolutely essential elements. If your bed is on the floor you may place the bank in the *hsun* position of your bedroom as you complete the twenty-seven days of collecting coins. After the twenty-seven-day period, when you empower the money vessel at the completion of the process, have the feeling that the bank will continue to collect and attract wealth and that its presence will impart continued valuable knowledge about money. While it is forbidden to spend any of the coins you are to collect, if an emergency arises and you need to use a coin of that denomination, do not use one that you have already put aside. Rather get change for that special purpose. Afterwards, on that day, for each coin of the chosen denomination you were forced to use, replace each coin with nine coins of the same denomination and put these together with the other chosen coins of that day in your bank.

If you need to travel during the twenty-seven days of collection you may take the piggy bank with you and set it up temporarily where you are staying, or more simply, bring a special purse with you, collect the coins in it, and upon your return home deposit them in your great wealth accumulator. If a husband and wife perform this method together the effectiveness will be even stronger. If you miss a day in carrying out this method, leave the old piggy bank where you placed it. Buy another one and start the whole process again.

## BORROWING MONEY *CHI* FROM SUCCESSFUL BUSINESSES BY COLLECTING WATER

This method involves collecting water from successful enterprises in order to borrow and make use of the *chi* of business success. You need to acquire a small new empty bottle and a vase to contain the water you will gather.

The basic procedure involves placing the vase in the *hsun*, or Wealth–related, position of your bedroom. Every day, for nine consecutive days, go to one successful business and collect some water from a water source on the premises and place it in the empty bottle. Bring the water home and pour it into the vase in your bedroom. Empower this action with the Three Secret Reinforcements, visualizing that the water in the vase is turning into money that bountifully will enter your life. Collect at least 2 tablespoons of water each day in the empty bottle. Choose successful banks, hotels, financial institutions, or other thriving businesses. Don't get water from private homes or religious institutions.

An alternative procedure involves keeping the vase in the kitchen near the stove. Acquire water from nine successful businesses on one auspicious day during the 11 A.M. - 1 P.M. period. The following morning take a little water from the vase, pour it into your hands, and rub your hands together while uttering the Six True Words mantra, OM MA NI PAD ME HUM, visualizing that the water is turning into money coming into your hands. Repeat this process of pouring water into your hands and rubbing them together for nine days. Rubbing the hands together is the body secret. The mantra is the speech secret. The visualization of water turning to money is the mind secret.

For either of these methods it is best if the water is gathered without creating a disturbance. Asking a bank teller or manager for water is an act some people might find challenging, especially if your money is not deposited in that bank. If you can do this calmly and smoothly that is excellent. Otherwise get the water from a water fountain or even from the bathroom. From a restaurant getting coffee or tea will also be an effective alternative. However, there is the danger in that case that the money that comes to you might not be so clean; that is to say, it might come from a corrupt source. If you practice this method on a weekend go to a place like a large active hotel. Do not use your own money to buy water.

These two methods of using water to borrow the *chi* of a successful business differ somewhat. We can compare them to two dishes of food. One dish may contain fried rice; another dish may contain noodles. These methods vary but both will nourish you.

## CREATING OPPORTUNITIES AND RECOGNITION

The two methods described here create a flow of *chi* that can greatly augment opportunities, recognition, business success, and social life. In creating this flow, it is important not to cut the movement we intentionally create. If, in contacting an individual, you are invited to lunch, have a tendency to say yes. If you are offered an opportunity after enacting either of the methods described, try to agree even if the financial return may not be optimal. The fortunate possibility you assent to may create other greater benefits.

## ADJUSTING THE *CHI* OF MOVING WATER TO ADVANCE CAREER AND SOCIAL LIFE

Moving water has to do with career, business, social life, and cash flow. It refers to the social context, the ocean of people in which we swim. Adjusting moving water is a personal *chi* adjustment method that can invigorate your business and create a wider social sphere.

Each day for twenty-seven consecutive days, contact at least one person known to you but with whom you have had no contact for the past six months. The contact may be in person, by phone, letter, fax, or e-mail. In each contact avoid uttering complaints or making any request. Do not turn down opportunities that arise from the communication. Visualize that your social activities, career, friendships, and the relationship between your private and your public life become balanced and harmonious. Reinforce each contact with the Three Secret Reinforcements, visualizing in detail your *chi* of moving water coming into a perfect balance for your unique individuality.

An **alternative method** is to meet nine new people a day for nine consecutive days. Be sure to exchange names. Reinforce the contact with the Three Secret Reinforcements to adjust your moving water.

In carrying out this adjustment of the *chi* of moving water be certain to miss no day in the sequence. If you do miss a day, you need to start over from the beginning. For the first variant described, if you meet an individual on the supermarket line, at a party, or visiting someone in a hospital and exchange names this contact can count as one of the needed ones for that day. It is much better to contact a greater number of people each day. I usually recommend that clients contact three people a day from their past. Many people have the reaction that this may be impossible. However, when they begin to make a list of people, they find that contacting eighty-one people over twenty-seven days is not impossible. The experiential dimension of adjusting moving water often involves an increase in social courage. As you near completion of this method, you may be able to contact people you were afraid to contact when you began.

## Mirrors in *Kan* and *Li*

On an auspicious day, in the 11 A.M. to 1 P.M. time period, place in your bedroom two small one-sided mirrors on the walls of the room two to three inches below the ceiling. Place one mirror in the *kan* position and the other mirror in *li* position. The mirrors should align exactly with each other so that the mirrors produce an infinite doubling of the image of each other. *Li* has to do with recognition, reputation, and fame, the realm of how we are seen; *kan* has to do with opportunities and social development. Empower this installation to create infinite opportunities and recognition. More opportunities will lead to greater recognition and an improved reputation. More recognition will create further opportunities. Reinforce with the Three Secret Reinforcements.

## FENG SHUI SECRETS OF LOVE, MARRIAGE, AND FAMILY

### ATTRACTING A NEW ROMANCE: THE HAIRSTYLE METHOD

Every third day change your hairstyle. Empower the changed hairstyle to create a dynamic that will help you develop a new romantic involvement. Repeat this method five times over fifteen days. Empower each change of hairstyle with the Three Secrets, visualizing that the transformation of your appearance removes obstacles to romance and attracts a person who will appropriately fulfill you needs. Visualize in detail about what you want but be general in terms of appearance and physical type.

## RECEIVING AUSPICIOUS MARRIAGE *CHI*

This method is excellent for someone hoping to get married. It is also good for those who wish to better an existing marriage.

Meet someone who has been married in the last three months. Take nine objects that you carry every day—keys, watch, wallet, rings, necklaces, credit cards—and wrap them in a red cloth. Request that the newlywed bride or groom handle your objects, shaking them or touching each object. Visualize that these objects receive happy, peaceful, and romantic marriage *chi* and that when the objects are returned to you, this *chi* comes into your life. Bring the objects back to your bedroom and place them overnight in the *kun* (Marriage) position. Use the Three Secrets, visualizing that the *chi* of successful marriage enters your life and helps you to get married or strengthen your existing marriage.

## MAINTAINING FAMILY UNITY: THE PHOTO AND STRING SECRET METHOD

Take photos of yourself and your spouse and position them facing each other. If you have children you may place photos of them between the photos of husband and wife. Expose these pictures to the moon between 11 P.M. and 1 A.M. with an awareness that the old man in the moon who presides over marriages and family life is blessing you and that the *ling chi* of happy marriage and family unity is entering into the photos. As you do this, wind a red string around the pictures ninety-nine times. Place the wrapped photos in a red envelope. Reinforce this action with the Three Secrets, intending that family unity or successful marriage will be strengthened.

Next day, during the same time period, bring the envelope to a source of moving water, like a river or the ocean, and throw the envelope in the water. Use the Three Secret Reinforcements with the intention that whatever the exigencies of time your relationship will be strong, secure, and durable, and that your family will abide in peace and unity. Alternatively you may place the photos in the soil of a potted, lively, luxuriant plant. This method is effective in keeping families together and in strengthening family unity.

## CONTROLLING AN UNRULY CHILD

A disobedient, unruly child, or a child of bad temperament, can be controlled by a special method that uses a nine-inch-long string. Place the string between your box spring and mattress for nine or twenty-seven days. Use the Three Secret Reinforcements with the intention that the string will acquire your *chi* and be able to energetically represent you. Take the string out and sew three inches of the string into the child's clothing. Retain the six-inch segment and wrap it around your little finger, visualizing that disobedience and difficult behavior will be controlled and diminished to the benefit of all concerned. Reinforce with the Three Secrets.

If a child of bad temperament wears green, his or her anger may be increased. For an angry and stubborn child, adding white to his or her clothing may weaken stubbornness. For a dishonest child, use green as a predominant color for the child's room or clothing. Empower this action to increase the influence on the child of the virtue of the Wood element (benevolence, compassion, and human heartedness).

## PROTECTION WHEN TRAVELING

### PROTECTING YOUR CAR

A crystal ball hung with a red string from your rearview mirror can be empowered to provide peacefulness in driving situations and protection against accidents. Remember to use the Three Secret Reinforcements. You may add beads placed on the string above the crystal in the colors associated with the Six True Words so that the power of this prayer enhances protection, comfort, and smooth circumstances while driving.

### THE MAGIC CARPET METHOD FOR A SUCCESSFUL JOURNEY

Acquire a six-foot-long red carpet. The carpet can be of a very thin material for ease of transport. As you are about to depart from your home on a potentially difficult journey lay the carpet across the threshold so that three feet are within the house and three feet are outside. Walk on the carpet as you depart using the Three Secrets, visualizing that your journey will be safe and that any untoward circumstances will be resolved without your coming to harm. Then roll the carpet up and throw it back inside your house. If you are going on a journey where there will be stays in different locations and then movement to new destinations you may bring the carpet with you or, having

235

thrown the carpet inside the house, bring a second carpet with you for use on your journey.

## CONCLUSION

In these pages I have endeavored to provide you with some tools that can change your life. We can use Feng Shui to increase the balance and harmony of our lives in unity with the Tao and with the universal *chi* we share with the cosmos, other people, our homes, workplaces, and the living Earth.

May this book lead you along the path which brings all beings happiness!

# BIBLIOGRAPHY

Feuchtwang, Stephen **An Anthropological Analysis of Chinese Geomancy** Vithagna Editions, Laos, 1974.

Groves, Derham **Feng Shui and Western Building Ceremonies**, Graham Brash, Singapore, 1991.

Lip, Evelyn **Feng Shui: Environments of Power A Study of Chinese Architecture**, Academy Editions, Great Britain, 1995.

Rossbach, Sarah **Interior Design with Feng Shui**, E.P. Dutton, New York, 1987.

Rossbach, Sarah **Feng Shui: The Chinese Art of Placement**, E.P. Dutton, New York, 1983.

Rossbach, Sarah and Lin Yun **Living Color: Master Lin Yun's Guide to Feng Shui and the Art of Color**, Kodansha International, New York, 1994.

Too, Lillian **The Complete Illustrated Guide to Feng Shui**, Element Books, Rockport, Maine, 1996.

Walters, Derek **Chinese Geomancy**, Element Books, Great Britain, 1989.

Wong, Eva **Feng Shui: The Ancient Wisdom of Harmonious Living For Modern Times**, Shambhala, Boston, 1996.


OTHER ASIAN AND WESTERN SOURCES

Hippocrates **On Airs, Waters, and Places Hippocratic Writings**, Great Books of the Western World vol. 10, Encyclopedia Brittanica, Inc., Chicago, 1952.

Michell, John **The Dimensions of Paradise: The Proportions and Symbolic Numbers of Ancient Cosmology**, Thames and Hudson, London, 1988.

Pennick, Nigel **The Ancient Science of Geomancy: Man in Harmony with the Earth**, Thames and Hudson, London, 1978.

Sung, Edgar **Classic Chinese Almanac: Year of the Tiger 1998**, MJE Publications, San Francisco, CA, 1998.

Sung, Edgar **The Practical Use of the Chinese Almanac: A Guide**, MJE Publishing, San Francisco, CA, 1996.

Trungpa, Chogyam **Shambala: The Sacred Path of the Warrior**, Bantam Books, New York, 1985.

Vitruvius **The Ten Books on Architecture** trans Morris Hicky Morgan, Dover Publications, New York, 1960 (1914).

Wharton, Edith and Ogden Codman **The Decoration of Houses**, W.W. Norton and Company, New York and London, 1978 (1902).

FENG SHUI SUPPLIES:
(Feng Shui Adjustment items that are GEO approved for correctness)
The Fen Shui Emporium, P.O. Box 6701, Charlottesville, VA 22901, Phone: 804-974-1726. E-mail: HYPERLINK mailto:clover@luckycat.com clover@luckycat:com  Website: http:www.luckycat.com

MJE Enterprises 2578 Noriega Street #203, San Francisco, CA 94122, Phone: 415-681-1182, Fax 415-681-1184 E-mail: HYPERLINK mailto:mjep2578@aol.com  mjep2578@aol.com

FENG SHUI EDUCATIONAL AND CONSULTING SERVICES:
**GEO Geomancy / Feng Shui Education Organization** 2939 Ulloa Street, San Francisco, CA 94116, Phone: 415-753-6408 Fax 415-753-1186. E-mail HYPERLINK mailto:FngshuiGEO@aol.com FngshuiGEO@aol.com Website: http://www.lapage.com/geo

YUN LIN TEMPLE
Yun Lin Temple
2959 Russell St.
Berkeley, CA 94705
(510) 841-2347

Yun Lin Monastery
2 Wheatley Rd.
Old Westbury, NY 11568
(516) 626-7799

http://www.yunlintemple.org
e-mail: yunlintemple@msn.com

# SUMMARY

## FRONT MATTER

## PART I: INTRODUCTION TO FENG SHUI  1

## PART II: FENG SHUI AT HOME AND WORK  97

## ABOUT THE AUTHOR

A disciple and senior student of Professor Thomas Lin Yun, Steven Post was the first person to teach Feng Shui in the United States and has been a consultant, educator, and writer on Feng Shui for almost 30 years. He is a co-founder of GEO, Geomancy/Feng Shui Education Organization. GEO is authoritative in Feng Shui education and consulting and conducts a three-year Professional Training Program, the most extensive and rigorous program in the world. He is an expert in multi-cultural Feng Shui knowledge including: Jewish, Japanese, European, and Great Goddess traditions. In addition to his column "Intercultural Geomancy," other books by Steven Post include: *The Geomancy of Ancient Crete, Walking and Christianity, Walking and the Military, Secrets of the Earth and Magic on the Basepaths.*

## ABOUT THE PHOTOGRAPHER

Mert Carpenter of Los Gatos, California, former Peace Corps volunteer, engineer, writer, and teacher, now specializes in industrial and architectural location photography (interiors and exteriors) nationwide. His wide experience, unique vision and relaxed demeanor have helped him work with people and the camera to make abstract ideas visual and the visual, dramatic.